SIN: Reality, Principle & Remedy

Other Books by Paul M. Ethington:

THE BATTLE: Powers and Principalities in the Struggle for the Souls of Men

GOD WITH US: Christ in Type, Form & Prophecy in the Old Testament

THE UNIQUELY CHRISTIAN WORLDVIEW

BLESSED! : Forget Not All His Benefits

CROUCHING AT THE DOOR: Sin and the Life of Holiness

THE UNFOLDING REVELATION OF PRAYER: A Bible Study

GOD'S TERRIFYING WARNING: His Mercy and His Judgment

THE MIRACLE OF THE SCRIPTURES: A Layman's Introduction to God's Word

THE LAST DAYS BEFORE FOREVER: A Biblical Eschatology

STUMBLING BLOCK OR CORNERSTONE: Essays and Poems on the Christian Life

THE INEVITABLE: Honest Talk about Death

UNHOLY DOMINION: Is It Really Christ's Church?

MAJESTY: Glory, Honor & Power

SIN

Reality, Principle & Remedy

Paul M. Ethington

Dedicated to Col. Charles Overstake of the Salvation Army under whom my father Oakley Ethington was sanctified at age 17 and who found a home to sing and to preach in the Church of the Nazarene. Whether Salvation Army, Church of the Nazarene, or others, the message of holiness was preached and lived which penetrated my heart. It is not only the preaching but the sweet aroma of sanctified lives including Oakley Ethington, Dora Bohlke, Janice Crawford, Nicholas Saucedo, Emma Murphy and my wife, Maria Ethington, to name but a few. To their influence along with that of the Holy Spirit I owe my deep faith.

TABLE OF CONTENTS

FORWARD

When SIN has hatched its best version of 'ME' and I find that I am still empty and needy, I then have a wonderful opportunity to recognize my Creator calling me. As you read this book, you will review the sinful fall of man beginning with Adam and on through time. Each of us has an opportunity to explore our own lives. Sin, its reality, principle and remedy is elaborated well as Paul Ethington faithfully has established every premise through the Word of God. He states "God intends us to be clean, to be separated unto holiness. When He does this work in us, He also exonerates us from judgment, rescues us from death and darkness and introduces us to light and life."

Because of mankind's very nature each of us has, from the beginning, wanted to explore good and evil. This deceives us into believing that we can be our own master and thus, in a way, our own god. But scripture tells us: "*For the wrath of God is revealed from heaven against all ungodliness and unrighteousness of men, who suppress the truth in unrighteousness, because what may be known of God is manifest in them, for God has shown it to them*" (Rom 1:18-20). So, we continue to seek answers as we find that we cannot save ourselves. We are a fallen race in need of God. In the power and authority that only He can give, we find grace that comes through our faith in a loving God. Embedded in our spirit is a desire to be fully reconciled to Him in a forever relationship.

Sin and salvation are not in a make-believe kingdom where mischief can be played with by resetting our own rules until we win. But rather it is a matter of entering the Kingdom of God by humbly knowing we have no answers that will open the gate to healing and transformation from our miserable fallen ways. He opens the gate of mercy. He brings joy and peace. The veil which hides this opportunity is our fallen estate, our sin.

By digesting this reading, we can come to realize the power of truth in the written words of God. It is not by way of the opinion of any man that we succeed in the pursuit of our redemption and sanctification. It is by way of our Holy God who can cause us to separate ourselves from sin and thrive in our relationship with Him.

It is a fearful thing that we do when we seek the favor of the Almighty. The journey of the heart toward salvation and a sanctified relationship with God is not a one-time commitment but is a commitment for life. The promises and faithfulness that you expect from God must also be a matter of your promise and faithfulness to Him. So, we are expected to do His will every day.

I am richer for having read this book.

James O. Ethington

PREFACE

Bear with me while we take a glimpse into the dark depths of what God sees, at what grieves and provokes Him, at some symptoms and manifestations of this hateful thing called sin, which stirred His heart of infinite love and pity and holiness to make such sacrifice to save sinners. – Samuel Logan Brengle

I value a few older books in my library. The one which I quote from above was written in 1934, acquired by Charles Overstake in 1935, marked in by him as he studied what Brengle had written, then given to my father, Oakley Ethington, in 1982 who studied and marked in it, and finally acquired by me after my dad's death in 1990. It now shows the notes and marks of three men. It has gotten the mileage it deserves and presents clearly a theology of love in the context of the Salvation Army in which my dad was sanctified.

I am convinced that most do not have a good concept of the depth and seriousness of sin, neither their own or others. For that reason they do not have a clear concept of the power of the cross of Jesus which overcame the terrible dread. Sin leads to death, but the cross brings everlasting life. This is not hyperbole!

My sin – O the bliss of this glorious tho't
My sin – not the part, but the whole
Is nailed to His cross, and I bear it no more!
Praise the Lord, praise the Lord, O my soul!

Personally, I have spent the better part of my life taking the gift of God for granted. I never thought my own sin was all that bad and God would just forgive me easily. I thought I had little from which to repent. Sensitivity to the convicting Holy Spirit has shown me something different. The last book I was able to publish called "Majesty" helped me to realize the immensity of the Creator of the universe (though the concept is difficult for my tiny finite mind to grasp). He is a jealous God. He is a holy God. He is righteous and just. He is patient, slow to anger, merciful and gracious. He has given us free moral agency, but in the end does not tolerate sin.

But I will show you whom you should fear: Fear him who, after your body has been killed, has authority to throw you into hell. Yes, I tell you, fear him! (Luke 12:5 NIV) – Jesus

The Bible gives us a picture of hell: *The Son of man shall send forth his angels, and they shall gather out of his kingdom all things that offend, and them which do iniquity; and shall cast them into a furnace of fire: there shall be wailing and gnashing of teeth* (Matt 13:41-42), *outer darkness* (Matt 25:30) and *everlasting punishment* (Matt 25:46).

It may be wrong to say that fear is the best motivator, although as a boy, more than once, I fled to the altar to repent. I will never forget reading Jonathan Edwards' "Sinners in the Hands of an Angry God" in American Literature as a junior in high school in 1963. His text was Deuteronomy 32:35: *To me belongeth vengeance and recompense; their foot shall slide in due time: for the day of their calamity is at hand, and the things that shall come upon them make haste.* These sermons were more prevalent during the great revivals of the last two centuries. Though fear causes an immediate *response, one can renege on his repentance once the fear subsides.*

What then causes a person to be drawn to repentance other than the convicting Holy Spirit and the choice each one of us must make? We must sense our awful and dangerous estate before God. We all must confess before God that we are sinners, prone to sin, who need a Savior. There are no short cuts, no other way given to man, except to come to the cross.

At the Cross

Isaac Watts, 1707

Thus might I hide my blushing face
While Calv'ry's cross appears
Dissolve my heart in thankfulness
And melt mine eyes to tears.
But drops of grief can ne'er repay
The debt of love I owe
Here, Lord, I give myself away
'Tis all that I can do

Here Isaac Watts expresses the clear truth: "'Tis all that I can do." With that in mind I have attacked the sin problem on three fronts: Part I is devoted to describing "The Reality of Sin." How should it be defined, avoided and talked about. What are its effects? In Chapter 5 we have attempted to provide a rather comprehensive listing of sins as described in the Bible. But there seems to be no bottom to this list. We would never be able to avoid all of these pitfalls, snares and quicksand of opportunity to fall and to fail. Part II for that reason describes "The Sin Principle." What underlies all of this tendency to sin, and what can set us free? Finally Part III puts forward "The Remedy" given us by God to overcome sin. We must realize the depth and power of sin over us, we must accept and believe the grace offered which separates us from sin, we must respond by faith in works which express our thanksgiving for release from the prison of our sins. And, we must be separate from the world and its loves, separated unto God and made clean by His call to holiness of heart and life. This divine purpose leads to full salvation. We will pray like David for a clean heart, made steadfast by His Spirit within. We will experience the joy of knowing and following Jesus. We will be upheld by His generous Spirit. We will be empowered to "teach transgressors God's way, and sinners will be converted to Him" (Psalm 51).

PART I
THE REALITY OF SIN

CHAPTER 1
WHY CAN'T I BE GOOD?
(The Inner Struggle)

The young atheist graduate student sat across from us in discussion of his beliefs (or absence of belief). How do you know right from wrong we asked; how do you know what is good? What is your standard of measure and authority? He answered, "I'm confident that I will know the difference when I see it. Ultimately, I will ask Does it do harm or not? Does it improve the quality of lives or does it make them worse?" That of course is an expression of secular humanism in a world without God. He, himself, will be the measure of sin or goodness. Only deep naivete' could hold such a position very long because life teaches us quite the opposite. The prophet Amos asked, "Can two walk together unless they be agreed?" The difficulty of the social contract can be summed up by Rodney Allen King's desperate question: "Can't we just all get along?" The answer is no we cannot if there is no standard outside ourselves to give us guidance. After his 15 minutes of fame and ill-gotten gains, he was found floating face-down in his swimming pool with no answer to his furtive question, no anchor, no lasting purpose, no direction and no salvation from his problems. In our social contract we legislate to rid ourselves of chaos. However, it is insufficient for us.

God has given us the Mosaic Law, and while necessary for us to understand sin, it cannot save us. Paul writes,

I was alive once without the law, but when the commandment came, sin revived and I died. And the commandment, which was to bring life, I found to bring death. For sin, taking occasion by the commandment, deceived me, and by it killed me. Therefore the law is holy, and the commandment holy and just and good. Has then what is good become death to me? Certainly not! But sin, that it might appear sin, was producing death in me through what is good, so that sin through the commandment might become exceedingly sinful. For we know that the law is spiritual, but I am carnal, sold under sin. For what I am doing, I do not understand. For what I will to do, that I do not practice; but what I hate, that I do. If, then, I do what I will not to do, I agree with the law that it is good. But now, it is no longer I who do it, but sin that dwells in me. For I know that in me (that is, in my flesh) nothing good dwells; for to will is present with me, but how to perform what is good I do not find. For the good that I will to do, I do not do; but the evil I will not to do, that I practice. Now if I do what I will not to do, it is no longer I who do it, but sin that dwells in me (Rom 7:9–20).

The battle with the law is a struggle within, because our nature has not changed. It is carnal, earthly, fleshly and powerless to keep God's law. This is similar to pulling ourselves up by our own bootstraps or blowing on the sail of our little bark and finding it will not move (I could explain that in terms of the physics, but I think we all know by our own experience). Jeremiah asked, "Can an Ethiopian change his skin or the leopard its spots? Then may you also do good who are accustomed to do evil" (Jer 13:23). Not likely! It was Israel's choice to continue in the sin that led to their captivity. They could not both "do good" and continue in their "lustful neighings, the lewdness of their harlotry, the abominations on the hills and fields." God saw it all, He warned, and finally it was too late. Here came the Assyrians and here came the Babylonians to inflict God's judgment.

There is a tremendous battle within, and I find myself divided, "wanting to do good but not able, instead doing the evil I hate. I cry out, "O wretched man that I am! Who will deliver me from this body of death?"

Cleanse Me
J. Edwin Orr, 1936

Cleanse me, O God, and know my heart today.
Try me, O Savior; know my thoughts, I pray.
See if there be some wicked way in me;
Cleanse me from ev'ry sin, and set me free.

CHAPTER 2
HOLINESS (The Divine Challenge)

We are to be like Jesus in our separation from the world, in purity, in love, and in the fullness of the Spirit. This is holiness – Samuel Logan Brengle [1]

To define holiness we find ourselves in contradistinction to sin; in defining sin we are describing the opposite of holiness. You say, "well only God could be holy." That would be true in my mind also had He not commanded us to be holy. Yet, the dynamic of holiness is much more than simply the absence of sin. Both must be talked about in the context of relational love. Sin is perverted love. Holiness is found in the love relationship with God.

Paul describes this sinless walk as "walking according to the Spirit rather than the flesh." We can be free from indwelling sin, but not if we try to conquer sin merely by our self-will and determination. There is a better way, a higher way which causes us to lean on Him rather than obsessing from our flesh and blood. Self-determination leads to death, while walking in the Holy Spirit leads to life and peace. This capability is because of the Spirit.

> *But if the Spirit of Him who raised Jesus from the dead dwells in you, He who raised Christ from the dead will also give life to your mortal bodies through His Spirit who dwells in you (Rom 8:11).*

Paul to the Galatians would say, "If we live in the Spirit, let us also walk in the Spirit (Gal 5:25)." So we can say that Holiness is a "highway". It is not for the unclean, but for the ransomed of the Lord. And, whoever walks on this highway, no matter how humble, will never go astray (Isa 35:8). You will not need a map to find your way, because your global positioning device will be the Holy Spirit.

We know about holiness only because God declares that He is holy. If we are ever to be holy ourselves, we must have some vision of the holiness of God. It is not at all necessary that we have a vision of the holiness of God as did Isaiah, but our spiritual eyes must be open to the glory and holiness of God. We must see Him not as "the man upstairs" or a "pal" on our level, but the God of the universe, the Creator of all things, our Father in heaven.[2] So our concept of holiness is defined in the holiness of God alone. When we start to say that the holiness of God and that of men and objects are two different things, we have muddied the waters. One such theologian used the phrase, "Our holiness is only in a relative sense." Of course there is no comparison in degree to the awe-inspiring transcendence of God in the brightness of His glory and moral purity, but we should not define men's holiness by man's limitation to be holy. If we are holy at all, it is the very holiness of God that makes us so!

> *"Speak to all the congregation of the people of Israel and say to them, You shall be holy, for I the LORD your God am holy* (Lev 19:2).
>
> *Consecrate yourselves, therefore, and be holy, for I am the LORD your God* (Lev 20:7).
>
> *You shall be holy to me, for I the LORD am holy and have separated you from the peoples, that you should be mine* (Lev 20:26).
>
> *You shall consecrate him [Aaron], for he offers the bread of your God. He shall be holy to you, for I, the LORD, who sanctify you, am holy* (Lev 21:8).

and you shall be to me a kingdom of priests and a holy nation.' these are the words that you shall speak to the people of Israel" (Exod 19:6).

Be ye therefore perfect, even as your Father which is in heaven is perfect (Matt 5:48).

Let us therefore, as many as be perfect, be thus minded: and if in anything ye be otherwise minded, God shall reveal even this unto you (Phil 3:15).

For God has not called us for impurity, but in holiness (1 Thes 4:7).

since it is written, "You shall be holy, for I am holy" (1 Pet 1:16).

"Be ye perfect" is usually equivocated as "mature" or "that which is brought to completion." That is what I have taught over the years, since the Greek can be interpreted this way. However, my argument for perfection would be the same as holiness. These are impossible human qualities that can only be attributed to God and His desire to make us so. Holiness, then, is purity of heart wrought by God who made us and recreates us in His own image.

Holiness requires a death to self (not a denial of the self as in Zen Buddhism), a setting aside of every encumbrance, and infilling with the presence of the Holy Spirit (He was with you, but will be in you), and a radical complete surrender and trust in Him. It is more than claiming Jesus as Lord; it is Jesus as Lord claiming you, all of you. Holiness begins and continues, then, with surrender.

Let's continue with the concept of "that which is brought to completion." What is it that is brought to completion? It is a fulfillment of purpose. The Holy Spirit's purpose becomes my purpose. His desire becomes my desire as expressed in Lillian Plankenhorn's 1946 little chorus:

> *My desire to be like Jesus*
> *My desire to be like Him*
> *His Spirit fill me, His love o'erwhelm me*
> *In deed and word To be like Him*

The wonderful sermon in print by Nina G. Gunter entitled *"Christian Perfection: Transformation to Wholeness"* explains this grace of holiness or perfection in a marvelous way. Her text was taken largely from Galatians Chapter 5. I quote much of the sermon here:[3]

> *When we are filled with the Spirit, we will bear "the fruit of the Spirit" (Gal 5:22). What is the fruit of the Spirit? What will our lives look like?*
>
> *We will be single-minded. We "will have no other mind" except the mind of Christ. Our one purpose, our whole aim, will be to love, please, and glorify the Lord.*
>
> *We will be servant-minded. We will not seek to dominate others, as "the flesh" would prompt us to do; instead, we will "through love serve one another." We will not force our personalities, our convictions, or our opinions on others. We will have the minds and hearts of servants, not tyrants.*
>
> *We will live peaceably. We will not "bite and devour one another." We won't chew each other out. The unity of the church will be precious to us, guarded by us.*
>
> *We will "walk in the Spirit" and not "fulfill the lust of the flesh."*

I am glad God offers us deliverance from life in the flesh. Too many people are living in bondage to their carnal selves. They struggle to overcome, but they don't see improvement. God alone can rescue you from yourself. Self-help efforts go only so far. Any attempt to overcome inward sin that bypasses the Cross will never resolve the problem.

Many people are allergic to themselves. When you are out of sorts with yourself, you will be out of sorts with everybody else. There is deliverance from that kind of bondage and frustration. Holiness is the solution for personal wholesomeness. Holiness is a relationship with Christ to be enjoyed.

Not only are we called to be a Holiness people, but also we are called to be a holy people. That means we will be different in our values, different in our conversations, different in our habits, and different in our relationships. Jesus didn't look different from other men, but He thought, spoke, and acted differently than them. Holy people, striving to be Christ like, will certainly be different.

On the positive side, when the Spirit of the Lord claims us and fills us, our love is made perfect. Our lives produce "the fruit of the Spirit" – "love, joy, peace, longsuffering, kindness, goodness, faithfulness, gentleness, self-control." Holiness makes Christianity beautiful.

What kind of perfection was Jesus talking about when He said, "Therefore you shall be perfect?" What Jesus had been talking about was love. He told His disciples to love their enemies, to return blessing for cursing, good for evil, and prayer for persecution. When smitten, they were to turn the other cheek, not strike back. Uncle Bud Robinson used to say, "Slap a sanctified person on the cheek, and you get honey all over your hand. and then you get under such conviction, you go back and ask the sanctified person to pray for you!"

Living out the Sermon on the Mount calls for the perfection of love. If you are asked to go a mile, you go an extra mile. You don't neglect anyone in need, and you don't play favorites. You love and forgive and you keep on loving and forgiving, because you want to be like Jesus Christ. Christlikeness is the standard for a holiness lifestyle.

What was Christ like? Peter tells us that "Christ also suffered for us, leaving us an example, that you should follow His steps: 'Who committed no sin, nor was guile found in His mouth;' who, when He was reviled, did not revile in return; when He suffered, He did not threaten, but committed Himself to Him who judges righteously."

We should have no hidden agendas. We should make no threats. We should not respond to evil with evil.

Perfect love purifies our motives. Perfect love is purity of intentions, not perfection of performance. The sanctified person does not intend to do evil or harm to anyone.

Perfect love is loving God with all of your heart, soul, mind and strength, and loving your neighbor as yourself. In loving people, you love their Creator. We are commanded to love one another as Christ has loved us. The crucifixion of self, the cleansing of the heart, empowers such love.

The love-mastered life is a wonderful life. You die to sin and self and all that Satan has to offer. You know that a new owner has taken over. You recognize that you are no longer your own. You aren't making the calls in your life anymore. You are allowing God to direct your steps.

Have you died to your carnal self? Can you testify with the apostle Paul, "I have been crucified with Christ; it is no longer I who live, but Christ lives in me"? When you die, there will be a resurrection. You will become a different person under the Lordship of Jesus Christ.

You can become identified with Christ. It seems to me that very few Christians ever get out of themselves and into Christ. They live a changed life but don't go on for the exchanged life. When you give your life and you take on the likeness of Jesus Christ, then you can say, "Not I, but Christ lives in me."

Have you died? If you will die, you won't die. If you wouldn't die you will die. Holiness is death to self. It is not the death of self. That's important to understand. Seeking heart purity and perfect love, we present ourselves to God as living sacrifices, not dead ones. You still live. You still have your distinct personality. You'll ask the Holy Spirit to modify it. Some say, "I can't help the way I am." No, you can't, but God can. You are changeable. The Lord must occupy the throne of your heart, the control center of your life. He who calls us to empty ourselves fills us with Himself. When you realize this truth, it makes you wonder why everybody wouldn't want to be sanctified. Why wouldn't everyone want to live this kind of victorious life, a life of freedom and joy and victory!

This cleansing, this fullness, is the work of the Spirit. We do not work ourselves up to this. The Holy Spirit gives us peace. The Holy Spirit gives us patience. The Holy Spirit enables us to be gentle and kind. The Holy Spirit helps us to have self-control. The Holy Spirit loves through us. We cannot perfect ourselves. Christlikeness is not attained by human effort. We call this experience a work of grace, for grace is unmerited favor. Grace is also God's power. We are at the mercy of God for the Holy Spirit to do the work within us that we cannot do.

The highest level of Christian living is likeness to Christ. The lowest level of divine grace is wherever we are in our need and desire to be like Christ. John speaks of His fullness:

Of His fullness we have all received, and grace for grace"
(John 1:16).

Holiness, then, is perfection of our purpose in Him; it is our fervent desire to be like Jesus, and it His living in and through us to accomplish His purposes.

In recent years I have availed myself of the teaching of Diane Leclerk, Northwest Nazarene University, regarding holiness. She has produced the text *"Discovering Christian Holiness: The Heart of Wesleyan-Holiness Theology,"* 2010. In a recent seminar which I attended entitled "Holiness for the 21st Century," she defined holiness in terms of five key concepts: Purity, Perfection, Power, Character and Love. Here I will summarize the meaning of these words to "holiness:"

Purity

Holiness cannot merely be defined by that which we avoid or do not do. That belief pretty much sucks the lifeblood out of holiness. Mildred Bangs Wynkoop in her book, *A Theology of Love*, 1972, says that you cannot define holiness as the absence of sin as if it were a Platonic form.[4] Destructive behaviors keep us from running the race well, but we need to be purified in that we reflect the character of Jesus, to love as Jesus loved.

Perfection

Wesley used the phrase "Christian Perfection," a biblical word: "Be perfect as My Heavenly Father is perfect" (Matt 5:48). This is literally meant by Jesus. In the Greek the connotation is this, that a thing is perfect if it participates in the purpose for which it was created. Wesley said that this purpose was for relationship, to love the Lord our God with all of our heart, mind, soul and strength and our neighbor as ourselves. You can't do that on your own, only with sanctifying grace. We are sanctified in order to reach the goal of Holy living.

Power

To make a long story short, we associate ourselves with Acts Chapter 2, not as an event in history, but a belief that is normative. Pentecostal power is the power to be transformed from inside out. It is power to overcome sin and temptation; and it is power for service. Historically, we have not emphasized power in some of our evangelical churches because we were avoiding association with the Pentecostal "tongues" movement. However, the Pentecostals have correctly understood the meaning of Jesus' words, "You shall receive power when the Holy Spirit has come upon you; and you shall be witnesses to Me in Jerusalem, and in all Judea and Samaria, and to the end of the earth" (Acts 1:8).

Character

Character is something we constantly live into, e.g. kindness. If you are a kind person, and act unkindly, you are out of character. Ongoing or "progressive" sanctification (as described in the end of Romans 12) shows us that we are freer to do a thing because of habituation. So the spiritual disciplines must come into play.

Love

The juxtaposition of the terms *holiness* and *love*, together with a "personal relationship" puts a meaning to each term, as well as uniting them. This transforms them from mere abstract terms into dynamically biblical concepts.[5] We were created in the image of a loving God with the potential to love. Holiness and sanctification is the renewal of that image in us. *Agape* Love is a Man on a cross, a "cruciform love," the ability to give ourselves away. This is to humanize humans to dignify another human being even when it costs dearly.

Ultimately, we are set free to be wholly His disciples, doing the things that Jesus showed us, free from every encumbrance.

Holiness Unto the Lord

Leila N. Morris, 1900

Called unto holiness, Church of our God,
Purchase of Jesus, redeemed by His blood;
Called from the world and its idols to flee,
Called from the bondage of sin to be free.

Called unto holiness, children of light,
Walking with Jesus in garments of white;
Raiment unsullied, nor tarnished with sin;
God's Holy Spirit abiding within.

Called unto holiness, praise His dear name!
This blessed secret to faith now made plain:
Not our own righteousness, but Christ within,
Living, and reigning, and saving from sin.

Holiness unto the Lord is our watchword and song
Holiness unto the Lord as we're marching along.
Sing it, shout it, loud and long:
Holiness unto the Lord, now and forever.

CHAPTER 3
FREE MORAL AGENCY (Choice)

"God voted for me, the devil voted against me, and I cast the deciding ballot for myself." – Bud Robinson

I have given this doctrine its own chapter because it plays a huge role in our understanding of sin. Wherever there is sin, there is a directive from God to do or not do something. It began in the Garden of Eden with Adam and Eve: "Of every tree of the garden you may freely eat; but of the tree of knowledge of good and evil you shall not eat, for in the day that you eat of it you shall surely die." So, there was given a directive, a choice and a consequence for not obeying the directive. These three elements are present in every instance of sin: a commandment, an opportunity to choose, and a consequence. Here was given for all mankind free moral agency (or choice) to obey or not obey God. God gave us self-determination with regard to sin. It is clear that even fallen man has freedom of choice.

Norman Geisler's argument for free will is that God's commandments carry a divine "ought" for humans, implying that they can and should respond positively to His commands. The responsibility to obey God's commands entails the ability to respond to them by God's enabling grace. Furthermore, if humans are not free, but all their acts are determined by God, then God is directly responsible for evil, a conclusion that is clearly contradicted by Scripture: [6]

> You are of purer eyes than to behold evil, And cannot look
> on wickedness. Why do You look on those who deal
> treacherously, And hold Your tongue when the wicked
> devours A person more righteous than he? (Habakkuk 1:13).

<blockquote>Let no one say when he is tempted, "I am tempted by God"; for God cannot be tempted by evil, nor does He Himself tempt anyone. But each one is tempted when he is drawn away by his own desires and enticed. Then, when desire has conceived, it gives birth to sin; and sin, when it is full-grown, brings forth death (James 1:13-17).</blockquote>

On free will John Wesley wrote, "Indeed, if man were not free, he could not be accountable either for his thoughts, words, or actions. If he were not free, he would not be capable either of reward or punishment; he would be incapable either of virtue or vice, of being either morally good or bad.[7]

Finally, that which is taught from the pulpit these days is that Christianity is based on a love relationship of God with humanity. If Man had no choice, there could not exist a love relationship.

Predestination is taught in Scripture, so all Bible-respecting Christians believe in some sort of predestination doctrine.

<blockquote>For whom He foreknew, He also predestined to be conformed to the image of His Son, that He might be the firstborn among many brethren. Moreover whom He predestined, these He also called; whom He called, these He also justified; and whom He justified, these He also glorified (Rom 8:29-30).</blockquote>

<blockquote>You did not choose Me, but I chose you and appointed you that you should go and bear fruit, and that your fruit should remain, that whatever you ask the Father in My name He may give you. These things I command you, that you love one another (John 15:16-17).</blockquote>

<blockquote>having predestined us to adoption as sons by Jesus Christ to Himself, according to the good pleasure of His will, In Him also we have obtained an inheritance, being predestined</blockquote>

according to the purpose of Him who works all things according to the counsel of His will (Eph 1:5,11)

to do whatever Your hand and Your purpose determined before to be done (Acts 4:28).

But we speak the wisdom of God in a mystery, the hidden wisdom which God ordained before the ages for our glory (1 Cor 2:7).

'*Predestine*' means "*to mark out beforehand.*" Christians hold differing views regarding what exactly is "marked out beforehand." Two major views have emerged with their variations:

Unconditional Predestination

John Calvin (1509-1564) continues to represent the position of much of Christianity today. The doctrine is often described in terms of the acronym, "T–U–L–I–P:"

Total **Depravity** (There is none who is good. Mark 10:18; Rom 3:9-10,18; Rom 8:7-8)
We ask, though man be depraved, does not God offer mercy and opportunity?
Unconditional **Election** (I will have mercy on whomever I will have mercy.) Rom 9:15)
We ask, does a man have a say in his salvation once grace is offered?
Limited **Atonement** ("to the men whom You have given Me..." John 17:6,9; 2 Cor 4:3)
We ask, are some men denied salvation from the beginning and for eternity? Did not Jesus die for all men in the same sense?
Irresistible **Grace** (No one can resist His will Rom 9:14-18)
We ask, is grace irresistible or is it invitational in nature?

<u>**Perseverance of the Saints**</u> (Nothing can separate us... Rom 8:39) We ask, does God alone determine who will endure to the end? Can a Christian lose his salvation (back-slide)? Why does the Bible even bother giving warnings?

To sum up the Calvinist position: *The absolute sovereignty of God and the complete depravity of man imply God's absolute predestination of man's eternal destiny.*

Conditional Predestination

James Arminius (1560–1609) taught that even though God knows how each of us will respond to His prevenient grace, He begins by decreeing that redemption is for all men. Secondly, His prevenient grace enables everyone who will to repent and believe. Thirdly, He receives all who repent and believe. Lastly, he saves or damns according to man's response, which is, of course, in accordance with His foreknowledge.

To sum up the Arminian position: *Men are born depraved with no inclination toward God. Yet, God extends prevenient grace which gives man free moral agency. Although God knows who ultimately will accept Him as Savior ("those he foreknew he also predestinated"), He extends the invitation to everyman with equal opportunity. His personal and relational covenant of grace leading to eternal life begins with the dictum, "Choose this day whom you will serve."*

Temporal Predestination is the view that predestination does not have to do with a pre-decision of God regarding the eternal destiny of people, but that it has to do with what God graciously decides for believers temporarily. J. Kenneth Grider in *A Wesleyan Holiness Theology* (1994) points out that the study of the six Greek instances of '*prooridzo*,' in the NT and other cognates in NT & OT show that

while God makes predecisions on various matters, they never have to
do with our eternal destiny. Rather, His predestination has to do
with His covenants with mankind (e.g. 1 Chron 16:15-17; Jer 31:31-34;
2 Cor 3:6-18).

Born to Be Damned? The Scriptures <u>do not</u> teach that God has
foreordained anyone to be damned:

> *Even so it is not the will of your Father who is in heaven
> that one of these little ones should perish (Matt 18:14).*

> *For God so loved the world that He gave His only
> begotten Son, that whoever believes in Him should not
> perish but have everlasting life. For God did not send His
> Son into the world to condemn the world, but that the
> world through Him might be saved (John 3:16-17).*

> *For this is good and acceptable in the sight of God our
> Savior, who desires all men to be saved and to come to
> the knowledge of the truth (1 Tim 2:3-4).*

> *The Lord is not slack concerning His promise, as some
> count slackness, but is longsuffering toward us, not
> willing that any should perish but that all should come
> to repentance (2 Pet 3:9).*

> *And the Spirit and the bride say, "Come!" And let him
> who hears say, "Come!" And let him who thirsts come.
> Whoever desires, let him take the water of life freely
> (Rev 22:17).*

But the Scriptures <u>do</u> affirm many other aspects of Christian
Doctrine:

- that the atonement is unlimited, as is the altogether-
  serious call to repent (Joel 2:13; Acts 17:30; 1 Pet 3:9);

- that God acts personally, is altogether just, and is unstintingly gracious (1 John 1:9);
- that real evil exists and is thwarting God's will (Matt 6:13; Rom 12:21; 1 Pet 5:8; John 8:44)
- that those who believe can fall from grace (2 Pet 2:20; Heb 4:6-11; 10:29; Rev 22:19);
- that salvation is by grace through faith (Eph 2:8-9);
- that Christ is our advocate (1 John 2:1);
- that we have a choice of allegiance (Rom 6:1-2; Luke 16:13);
- that repentance is required for forgiveness of sins (Acts 3:19);
- that we are to bear witness to the gospel (Acts 1:8);
- that we must open the door to Christ (Rev 3:20);
- that there are promises for the overcomer (Rev 3:21);
- that God calls us to holiness (James 4:8)

I Surrender All

Van DeVenter & Weeden, 1896

All to Jesus I surrender; all to Him I freely give.
I will ever love and trust Him, In His presence daily live.
I surrender all, I surrender all.
All to Thee my blessed Savior, I surrender all.

We believe that the position of "conditional/temporal predestination" best fits all Scriptural understanding. The following chart is used to describe these ideas and to show their interrelationships. No graphic is perfect, but I use this to teach the condition of man, the necessity of grace and the plan of salvation:

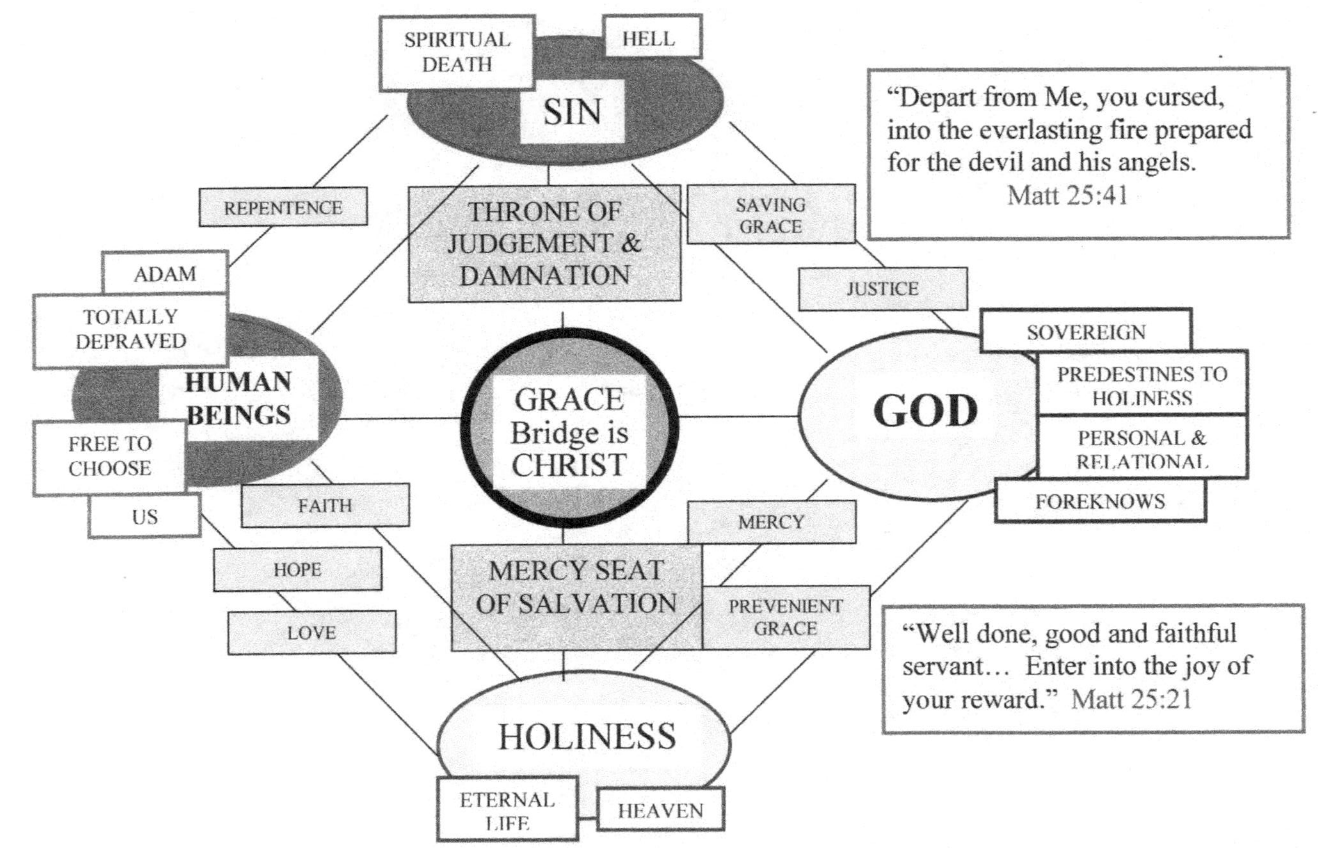
SPIRITUAL DEATH
HELL
SIN
"Depart from Me, you cursed, into the everlasting fire prepared for the devil and his angels.
Matt 25:41
REPENTENCE
THRONE OF JUDGEMENT & DAMNATION
SAVING GRACE
JUSTICE
ADAM
TOTALLY DEPRAVED
SOVEREIGN
PREDESTINES TO HOLINESS
HUMAN BEINGS
GRACE Bridge is CHRIST
GOD
PERSONAL & RELATIONAL
FREE TO CHOOSE
FOREKNOWS
US
FAITH
MERCY
HOPE
MERCY SEAT OF SALVATION
PREVENIENT GRACE
LOVE
"Well done, good and faithful servant… Enter into the joy of your reward." Matt 25:21
HOLINESS
ETERNAL LIFE
HEAVEN

CHAPTER 4
SIN IN A BOX (Classification)

"There are four kinds of sin: attitude, action, neglect and intent." – Ron Graham

In the effort to define and classify the huge list of sins that appear in the bible, there have been several attempts to group or classify them by category. One example is the Catholic church's definition of the so-called seven deadly sins.

"THE SEVEN DEADLY SINS:"

Greed	**Envy**	**Pride**	**Wrath**
Gluttony	**Sloth**	**Lust**	

vs. their opposite virtues:

Charity	**Kindness**	**Humility**	**Patience**
Temperance	**Diligence**	**Chastity**	

These do not even begin to cover the gamut of sins presented in the Bible. We have made an attempt to list the bulk of them in Chapter 5 ahead. There are several well-known definitions of sin. We mention some of them here:

<u>THE WILLFUL VIOLATION OF THE KNOWN LAW OF GOD IS SIN</u>

This seems reasonable, especially with regard to children who have not been taught right from wrong, good and evil. However, as an adult, can we claim exemption when we have ignored God's warnings, kept ourselves ignorant so to speak? No, we cannot.

LAWLESSNESS ("PASSING OVER" MY COVENANT)

Here we can include every sin made clear in the Bible. For example it includes The Ten Commandments of Exodus 20, all of those things listed that God hates, and all the sins we have listed in the next chapter. Included here is all of the ritual Mosaic law. This would include anything confirmed by Jesus and by apostolic authority.

MISSING THE MARK

It is because of this definition that Paul can say that "All have sinned and fallen short of the glory of God (Romans 3:23).

MISSING THE WAY (OMMISSION & AVOIDANCE)

A good example in Scripture of which we are aware is in the story of Samuel with reference to Eli whose sons were wicked and whom he made no attempt to stop: (God said to Samuel, "for I told Eli I would judge his family forever because of the sin he knew about [and did nothing about]" Eli's sons were "contemptible." Eli's sin was that he stood by and did nothing (He missed the way).

In the New Testament James 4:17 says *"To him that knoweth the right thing to do, and doeth it not, to him it is sin."*

WANDERING AWAY

This is going astray. It implies carelessness, forgetfulness & self-absorption.

*All we like sheep have gone astray; We have turned,
everyone, to his own way"* (Isa 53:6).

FALLING SHORT OF LOVE'S STANDARD

Jesus said "Thou shalt love..." (Matt 22:37-40).

Despite the definition which applies above, Isaiah goes on to say "The Lord has laid on Him (Jesus) the iniquity of us all." That is the good news.

Although most are ready to condemn others for their sin, many are the excuses for sin that keep men from confessing their need for a savior. These are rationalizations that will not wash with God:

1) "I didn't know any better."
     ...but God says, they are without excuse (Rom 1:18-20)

2) "I can't help myself."
     ...but God says, for each temptation there is a way of escape (1 Cor 10:13)

3) "I am socially or economically deprived."
     ...but God says, He is no respecter of persons (Acts 10:34)

4) "Everybody else is doing it."
     ...but God says, work out your own salvation (Phil 2:12)
     ...if the blind lead the blind, both will fall (Matt 15:14)

5) "The Devil made me do it."
     ...but God says,
     every man is responsible for his own sin (Phil 2:12)

...resist the devil and he will flee from you (James 4:7)

Despite these many excuses the Bible tells us that the wage of sin will be death

> *"The penalty of sin is that gradually you get used to it and do not know that it is sin."*- Oswald Chambers

> *"The wages of sin is death – thank God I quit before payday."* – Reamer Loomis

The results of sin are inevitable:

1) God's Displeasure
2) Guilt & Shame; Hiding, Secrecy, Covering Up
3) Restless, Dissatisfied Spirit
4) Dissipation; Bondage, Entrapment, Spiraling Downward, Habitual Grip
5) God's Judgment: Spiritual, Physical & Eternal Death

When evil prevails not only in individuals, but in large groups or organizations, we call it "systemic evil." The beauty of this from Satan's point of view is that no individual has to take the blame or feel responsible. "I was just taking orders," they might say, or since it is lawful and so many were doing it together, "I felt it was morally O.K." Sin spreads and entrenches itself until it institutionalizes in my home, my society, my nation, world trends, according to the "Prince of the power of the air."

> *And you He made alive, who were dead in trespasses and sins, in which you once walked according to the course of this world, according to the prince of the*

power of the air, the spirit who now works in the sons of
disobedience (Eph 2:1-2).

We are in a battle that is bigger than ourselves, a battle for the truth, a spiritual battle involving principalities, powers and rulers of the darkness. Satan wants us to identify with and to become dependent upon, his world system which enslaves us.

> *For we do not wrestle against flesh and blood, but*
> *against principalities, against powers, against the*
> *rulers of the darkness of this age, against spiritual hosts*
> *of wickedness in the heavenly place (Eph 6:12).*

The book of Revelation identifies this as "Mystery Babylon the Great, the Mother of Harlots and of the Abominations of the Earth" (Rev 17:5).

And I heard another voice from heaven saying, "Come out of her, my people, lest you share in her sins, and lest you receive of her plagues. For her sins have reached to heaven, and God has remembered her iniquities. Render to her just as she rendered to you, and repay her double according to her works; in the cup which she has mixed, mix double for her. In the measure that she glorified herself and lived luxuriously, in the same measure give her torment and sorrow; for she says in her heart, 'I sit as queen, and am no widow, and will not see sorrow.' Therefore her plagues will come in one day—death and mourning and famine. And she will be utterly burned with fire, for strong is the Lord God who judges her.... For in one hour such great riches came to nothing.' Every shipmaster, all who travel by ship, sailors, and as many as trade on the sea, stood at a distance and cried out when they saw the smoke of her burning, saying, 'What is like this great city?' "They threw dust on their heads and cried out, weeping and wailing, and saying, 'Alas, alas, that great city, in which all who had ships on the sea became rich by her wealth! For in one hour she is made desolate.' "Rejoice over her, O heaven, and you holy apostles and prophets, for God has avenged you on her!" ... And I heard, as it were, the voice of a great multitude, as the sound of many waters and as the sound of mighty thunderings, saying, "Alleluia! For the Lord God Omnipotent reigns! (Rev 18:4–8, 17–20; 19:6)

Having won the battle of inward sin (Rom 7–8), our battle with sin becomes outward and united with the kingdom of our Lord and of His Christ.

Let no one deceive you by any means; for that Day will not come unless the falling away comes first, and the man of sin is revealed, the son of perdition, who opposes and exalts himself above all that is called God or that is worshiped, so that he sits as God in the temple of God, showing himself that he is God. Do you not remember that when I was still with you I told you these things? And now you know what is restraining, that he may be revealed in his own time. For the mystery of lawlessness is already at work; only He who now restrains will do so until He is taken out of the way. And then the lawless one will be revealed, whom the Lord will consume with the breath of His mouth and destroy with the brightness of His coming. The coming of the lawless one is according to the working of Satan, with all power, signs, and lying wonders, and with all unrighteous deception among those who perish, because they did not receive the love of the truth, that they might be saved. And for this reason God will send them strong delusion, that they should believe the lie, that they all may be condemned who did not believe the truth but had pleasure in unrighteousness (2 Thes 2:3-12).

Especially pay attention to verse 8: *And then the lawless one will be revealed, whom the Lord will consume with the breath of His mouth and destroy with the brightness of His coming.*

The deception will be revealed; God will end it, and Satan, the man of sin and his desperate battle against God will come to an end.

A Mighty Fortress Is Our God
Martin Luther, 1529

And tho' this world, with devils filled,
Should threaten to undo us,
We will not fear, for God hath willed
His truth to triumph through us.
The prince of darkness grim –
We tremble not for him.
his rage we can endure,
For, lo, his doom is sure;
One little word shall fell him.

CHAPTER 5
EXACTLY WHAT DID I DO?
(A Listing of Specific Sins)

If we say that we have no sin,
we deceive ourselves, and the
truth is not in us - John

Sin is not merely an act. It is a state of the heart as well. Every sin is a sin against God and a blow against His righteous government and the safeguards He has thrown around His moral creation.[8] When Joseph in Egypt was tempted to commit adultery with Potiphar's wife, he resisted and overcoming temptation, he said, *"How then can I do this great wickedness, and sin against God?"* (Gen 39:9) When David was confronted by Nathan's "Thou art the man," He repented of his adultery with Bathsheba and murder of her husband. He prayed, *"Against Thee, Thee only, have I sinned, and done this evil in Thy sight"* (Psalm 51:4). Brengle uses the passage from Jesus *"When saw we Thee an hungered, or athirst, or a stranger, or naked, or sick, or in prison, and did not minister unto Thee? Then shall He answer them, saying, Verily I say unto you, inasmuch as ye did it not to one of the least of these, ye did it not to Me. And these shall go away into everlasting punishment: but the righteous into life eternal* (Matt 25:34-46). It is God's law that is broken. It is God's authority that is defied. It is God's holiness and justice that are despised. When a man sins, it is against God. Brengle goes on to say "Indeed, sin is nothing less than lawlessness – a huge selfishness – that amounts to moral and spiritual anarchy. The sinner would pull God off His throne and kill Him if he could."

We who have grown up with the Bible are used to them. Sometimes they are describing a single sin, other times a list of sins and their consequence. After reading them all, one is convinced that there is no bottom to this list. They create a temptation, for us to present a finite list of activities to avoid. We soon realize that there is no way for us to avoid all of them in life. There are too many and some so engrained that we have little hope of escape. However, they serve a purpose, and that is to show us a representation which is complete enough to give us an idea of that which condemns us.

Only some of the biblical references follow here. I have taken license to paraphrase many of these verses for the sake of presenting sins as a list. The length of this chapter testifies to the endless possibility for sins when expressed as individual acts. I list them here more or less in order of appearance in the Bible and have combined some verses for brevity.

There needs to be a distinction made between that which is determined as sin for all generations and peoples, and that given as Mosaic law for the ancient Hebrews. For example, I do not imagine you would think it righteous to put a son or daughter to death for parental disobedience (Deut 21:18-21) or for a hand to be cut off for a wife's grabbing of her husband's opponent's groin in a fight (Deut 25: 11-12). You probably should not think it a sin to eat pork or intermarry. Was the Inquisition righteous in putting witches (sorcerers) to death?(Exod 22:18). Because of Jesus' teaching, we would recoil at "an eye for an eye, a tooth for a tooth (Lev 24:19-20). However, any breaking of the Ten Commandments should be considered for all time and peoples (Exod 20:1-17; Deut 5:1-22). In fact if one uses the guideline of the Ten Commandments against which all of these sins can be found, whether direct equivalence, corollary or inference, one will not go wrong.

It should be said that for the Christian believer one needs to add the Sermon on the Mount and any apostolic instruction by association as sin. That would include directives to be holy as God is holy, for example putting on tender mercies, kindness, humility, meekness, and longsuffering (Colossians 3:12). Not doing these things constitutes sin because the believer knows better in most cases. I have not included "not doing these things" as part of this sin list. For that reason we present the following as representative though certainly not all-inclusive:

Genesis 39:7-9; Jeremiah 23:10

And it came to pass after these things that his master's wife cast longing eyes on Joseph, and she said, "Lie with me."... [But Joseph said,] "How then can I do this great wickedness, and sin against God?"... For the land is full of adulterers; For because of a curse the land mourns. The pleasant places of the wilderness are dried up. Their course of life is evil, And their might is not right.

- Adultery

Exodus 20:1-17

And God spoke all these words, saying "you shall not [commit these sins]:"

- Have other gods before Me
- Make a carved image and bow down to it
- Take the Lord's name in vain
- Ignore the Sabbath
- Dishonor your father and mother
- Murder
- Commit Adultery
- Steal
- Bear false witness
- Covet

Exodus 21:16

"He who kidnaps a man and sells him, or if he is found in his hand, shall surely be put to death.

- Kidnapping

Exod 21:22-25; Jeremiah 1:4-5; Psalm 127:3-5

If men fight, and hurt a woman with child, so that she gives birth prematurely... Before I formed you in the womb I knew you. Behold children are a heritage from the Lord.

- Murder of the unborn

Exod 22:22-24

You shall not afflict any widow or fatherless child. If you afflict them in any way, and they cry at all to Me, I will surely hear their cry; and My wrath will become hot, and I will kill you with the sword; your wives shall be widows, and your children fatherless.

- Afflicting a widow or fatherless child

Exodus 23:1,8

You shall not circulate a false report. Do not put your hand with the wicked to be an unrighteous witness.... And you shall take no bribe, for a bribe blinds the discerning and perverts the words of the righteous.

- Bearing False Witness
- Taking a bribe

Leviticus 18:22; Rom 1:24-28

You shall not lie with a male as with a woman; it is an abomination. Therefore God gave them up in the lusts of their hearts to impurity, to the dishonoring of their bodies among themselves, because they exchanged the truth about God for a lie and worshiped and served the creature rather than the Creator, who is blessed forever! Amen. For this reason God gave them up to dishonorable passions:

- Homosexuality
- Lesbianism

Leviticus 19:13

You shall not cheat your neighbor, nor rob him. The wages of him who is hired shall not remain with you all night until morning.

- Cheating or robbing your neighbor

Numbers 30:2

If a man makes a vow to the LORD, or swears an oath to bind himself by some agreement, he shall not break his word; he shall do according to all that proceeds out of his mouth.

- Breaking a vow

Deuteronomy 4:19; 17:1-7; Psalm 81:9; Acts 15:20

And take heed, lest you lift your eyes to heaven, and when you see the sun, the moon, and the stars, all the host of heaven, you feel driven to worship them and serve them, which the LORD your God has given to all the peoples under the whole heaven as a heritage. There shall be no foreign god among you; Nor shall you worship any foreign god.

- Idolatry

<u>**Deuteronomy 18:10–11; Leviticus 20:6; Isaiah 8:19; Isaiah 47:13**</u>

There shall not be found among you anyone who makes his son or his daughter pass through the fire, or one who practices witchcraft, or a soothsayer, or one who interprets omens, or a sorcerer, or one who conjures spells, or a medium, or a spiritist, or one who calls up the dead.... And the person who turns to mediums and familiar spirits, to prostitute himself with them, I will set My face against that person and cut him off from his people.... And when they say to you, "Seek those who are mediums and wizards, who whisper and mutter," should not a people seek their God? Should they seek the dead on behalf of the living?... You are wearied in the multitude of your counsels; Let now the astrologers, the stargazers, And the monthly prognosticators Stand up and save you From what shall come upon you.

Study of the occult:
- Make children pass through fire
- Witchcraft
- Seeking out a soothsayer
- Interpreting omens
- Sorcery
- Using conjures or spells
- Using a medium
- Calling on familiar spirits
- Calling up the dead
- Astrology

<u>**Deuteronomy 21:18–21**</u>

If a man has a stubborn and rebellious son who will not obey the voice of his father or the voice of his mother, ... shall take hold of him and bring him out to the elders of his city, to the gate of his city. And they shall say to the elders of his city, 'This son of ours is stubborn and rebellious; he will not obey our voice; he is a glutton and a drunkard.' Then all the men of his city shall stone him to death with stones; so you shall put away the evil from among you, and all Israel shall hear and fear.

- Parental disobedience

Deuteronomy 22:5

A woman shall not wear anything that pertains to a man, nor shall a man put on a woman's garment, for all who do so are an abomination to the LORD your God.

- Cross-dressing

Deuteronomy 22:5-27

But if a man finds a betrothed young woman in the countryside, and the man forces her and lies with her, then only the man who lay with her shall die. But you shall do nothing to the young woman; there is in the young woman no sin deserving of death

- Rape

Deuteronomy 27:20-23

Cursed *is* the one who lies with his father's wife, because he has uncovered his father's bed. Cursed *is* the one who lies with any kind of animal. Cursed *is* the one who lies with his sister, the daughter of his father or the daughter of his mother. Cursed *is* the one who lies with his mother-in-law.

- Incest
- Bestiality
- Adultery

Psalm 10:2-11

*The wicked in his pride persecutes the poor; For the wicked boasts of his heart's desire; He blesses the greedy and renounces the L*ORD*. The wicked in his proud countenance does not seek God; God is in none of his thoughts. His mouth is full of cursing and deceit and oppression; His eyes are secretly fixed on the helpless. That the helpless may fall by his* [f]*strength. He has said in his heart, "You will not require an account."*

- Persecutes the poor
- Proudly Boasts in his heart's desire
- Blesses the greedy
- Renounces the Lord
- Cursing and deceit
- Oppresses the helpless
- Does not think he will be held to account

Psalm 34:13

Keep your tongue from evil, And your lips from speaking deceit.

- Speaking evil of others
- Speaking deceitfully

Psalm 52:7

"Here is the man who did not make God his strength, But trusted in the abundance of his riches, And strengthened himself in his wickedness."

- Trusting in wealth & wickedness rather than God

Psalm 59:12

For the sin of their mouth and the words of their lips, Let them even be taken in their pride, And for the cursing and lying which they speak.

- Pride
- Cursing
- Lying

Psalm 101:5

Whoever secretly slanders his neighbor, Him I will destroy; The one who has a haughty look and a proud heart, Him I will not endure.

- Slander
- haughtiness
- proud heart

Proverbs 6:16-19

There are six things the LORD hates, seven that are detestable to him:

- haughty eyes
- a lying tongue
- hands that shed innocent blood
- a heart that devises wicked schemes
- feet that are quick to rush into evil
- a false witness who pours out lies
- stirring up conflict in the community.

Proverbs 14:21

He who despises his neighbor sins; But he who has mercy on the poor, happy is he.

- Despising the poor neighbor

Proverbs 27:4

Wrath is cruel and anger a torrent, but who is able to stand before jealousy?

- Wrath
- Anger
- Jealousy

Isaiah 5:20

Woe to those who call evil good, and good evil; Who put darkness for light, and light for darkness; Who put bitter for sweet, and sweet for bitter!

- Calling evil good, and good evil

Isaiah 30:1

Woe to the rebellious children," says the L*ORD,* *Who take counsel, but not of Me, And who devise plans, but not of My Spirit, That they may add sin to sin.*

- Taking ungodly counsel
- Devising plans not of God

Isa 47:13-14

Let now the astrologers, the stargazers and the monthly prognosticators stand up and save you from what shall come upon you. Behold, they shall be as stubble, the fire shall burn them; they shall not deliver themselves from the power of the flame.

- Astrology

Jeremiah 5:3-4

O L*ORD, are not Your eyes on the truth? You have stricken them, But they have not grieved; You have consumed them, But they have refused to receive correction. They have made their faces harder than rock; They have refused* *to return. Therefore I said, "Surely these are poor. They are foolish; For they do not know the way of the LORD, The judgment of their God.*

- Refusing to take correction

Jeremiah 16:12; 17:5
Each one follows the dictates of his own evil heart, so that no one listens to Me. Cursed is the man who trusts in man And makes flesh his strength, Whose heart departs from the LORD.

- Trusting in man rather than God

Habakuk 2:9
Woe to him who covets evil gain for his house, That he may set his nest on high, That he may be delivered from the power of disaster!

- Coveting evil gain

Malachi 2:16: Matthew 19:8-9
For the LORD God of Israel says that He hates divorce, For it covers one's garment with violence, Says the LORD of hosts. Therefore take heed to your spirit, That you do not deal treacherously.... He said to them, "Because of your hardness of heart Moses allowed you to divorce your wives, but from the beginning it was not so. And I say to you, whoever divorces his wife, except for sexual immorality, and marries another, commits adultery; and whoever marries her who is divorced commits adultery."

- Divorce (adultery)

Malachi 3:8-9

"Will a man rob God? Yet you have robbed Me! But you say, 'In what way have we robbed You?' In tithes and offerings. ⁹You are cursed with a curse, For you have robbed Me, Even this whole nation.

- Robbing God

Matthew 5:22

But I say to you that whoever is angry with his brother without a cause shall be in danger of the judgment. And whoever says to his brother, 'Raca!' shall be in danger of the council. But whoever says, 'You fool!' shall be in danger of hell fire.

- Angry with his brother without cause
- Calls his brother "fool"

Matthew 5:28

But I say to you that everyone who looks at a woman with lustful intent has already committed adultery with her in his heart.

- Looking at a woman with lustful intent

Matthew 6:1-4,16-18

"Take heed that you do not do your charitable deeds before men, to be seen by them... that your charitable deed may be in secret; and your Father who sees in secret will Himself reward you openly. *"Moreover, when you fast, do not be like the hypocrites, ...but to your Father who is in the secret place; and your Father who sees in secret will reward you openly.*

- Religious practice to be seen by men

<u>**Matthew 7:1-5**</u>
"*Judge not, that you be not judged... First remove the plank from your own eye, and then you will see clearly to remove the speck from your brother's eye.*"

- Judgement of others

<u>**Matthew 10:32-33**</u>
Therefore whoever confesses Me before men, him I will also confess before My Father who is in heaven. But whoever denies Me before men, him I will also deny before My Father who is in heaven.

- Denying Jesus before men

<u>**Matthew 15:7-9; 2 Tim 3:15**</u>
These people draw near to Me with their mouth, And honor Me with their lips, But their heart is far from Me. And in vain they worship Me, Teaching as doctrines the commandments of men.'...having a form of godliness but denying its power.

- Teaching others, but their hearts far from God

<u>**Matthew 15:19**</u>
For out of the heart proceed evil thoughts, murders, adulteries, fornications, thefts, false witness, blasphemies.

- Murders
- Adulteries
- Fornications
- Thefts
- False witness
- Blasphemies

Matthew 18:6; 1 Cor 8:9

But whoever causes one of these little ones who believe in Me to sin, it would be better for him if a millstone were hung around his neck, and he were drowned in the depth of the sea.... But beware lest somehow this liberty of yours become a stumbling block to those who are weak.

- Causing a weak believer to sin

Matthew 23:25

Woe to you, scribes and Pharisees, hypocrites! For you cleanse the outside of the cup and dish, but inside they are full of extortion and self-indulgence.

- Hypocrisy
- Extortion
- Self-indulgence

Mark 3:29

but he who blasphemes against the Holy Spirit never has forgiveness, but is subject to eternal condemnation

- Blasphemy against the Holy Spirit

Mark 7:21-23

For from within, out of the heart of man, come evil thoughts; all these evil things come from within, and they defile a person:

- Sexual immorality
- Theft
- Murder
- Adultery
- Coveting
- Wickedness

- Deceit
- Sensuality
- Envy
- Slander
- Pride

Mark 8:38

For whoever is ashamed of Me and My words in this adulterous and sinful generation, of him the Son of Man also will be ashamed when He comes in the glory of His Father with the holy angels."

- Ashamed of the gospel

Mark 10:11-12

So he said to them, "Whoever divorces his wife and marries another commits adultery against her. And if a woman divorces her husband and marries another, she commits adultery."

- Divorces and remarries

Mark 11:26

But if you do not forgive, neither will your Father in heaven forgive your trespasses."

- Unforgiveness

Luke 6:37

Judge not, and you shall not be judged. Condemn not, and you shall not be condemned. Forgive, and you will be forgiven

- Judgmental
- Condemning
- Unforgiving

Luke 9:23; 2 Corinthians 5:15

Then He said to them all, "If anyone desires to come after Me, let him deny himself, and take up his cross daily, and follow Me.... and He died for all, that those who live should live no longer for themselves, but for Him who died for them and rose again.

- Living for yourself

Luke 11:52; Mark 9:42

Woe to you lawyers! For you have taken away the key of knowledge. You did not enter in yourselves, and those who were entering in you hindered. But whoever causes one of these little ones who believe in Me to stumble, it would be better for him if a millstone were hung around his neck, and he were thrown into the sea.

- Prevent others from finding Christ

Luke 12:15

And He said to them, "Take heed and beware of covetousness, for one's life does not consist in the abundance of the things he possesses.

- Covetousness

Luke 12:45

But if that servant says in his heart, 'My master is delaying his coming,' and begins to beat the male and female servants, and to eat and drink and be drunk,

- Abuse to servants (employees)
- Drunkenness

Acts 7:51

You stiff-necked and uncircumcised in heart and ears! You always resist the Holy Spirit; as your fathers did, so do you.

- Resisting the Holy Spirit

Acts 8:23; Hebrews 12:15

For I see that you are poisoned by bitterness and bound by iniquity. Let all bitterness, wrath, anger, clamor, and evil speaking be put away from you, with all malice.

- Bitterness
- Wrath
- Anger
- Clamor
- Evil Speaking
- Malice (desire to see others suffer)

Romans 1:28-31

God gave them over to a debased mind, to do those things which are not fitting; being filled with all unrighteousness, sexual immorality, wickedness, covetousness, maliciousness; full of envy, murder, strife, deceit, evil-mindedness; they are whisperers, backbiters, haters of God, violent, proud, boasters, inventors of evil things, disobedient to parents,

- Sexual immorality
- Covetousness
- Maliciousness
- Envy
- Murder
- Strife
- Deceit
- Evil-mindedness

- Whisperers
- Backbiters
- Haters of God
- Violent
- Proud
- Boasters
- Inventors of evil things
- Disobedient to parents

Romans 3:13-18

Their throat is an open tomb; With their tongues they have practiced deceit; The poison of asps is under their lips"; Whose mouth is full of cursing and bitterness. Their feet are swift to shed blood; Destruction and misery are in their ways; And the way of peace they have not known. There is no fear of God before their eyes.

- Deceit
- Cursing
- Bitterness
- Swift to shed blood
- Way of destruction and misery
- No fear of God

Romans 8:6-8

For to be carnally minded is death, but to be spiritually minded is life and peace. Because the carnal mind is enmity against God; for it is not subject to the law of God, nor indeed can be. So then, those who are in the flesh cannot please God.

- Carnal mindedness

Romans 14:23

But whoever has doubts is condemned if he eats, because the eating is not from faith. For whatever does not proceed from faith is sin:

- Not acting from faith

Romans 13:13

Let us walk properly, as in the day, not in revelry and drunkenness, not in lewdness and lust, not in strife and envy.

- Revelry and Drunkenness
- Lewdness and Lust
- Strife and Envy

Romans 16:17

ow I urge you, brethren, note those who cause divisions and offenses, contrary to the doctrine which you learned, and avoid them.

- Cause divisions and offenses
- False Doctrine

1 Corinthians 6:9-11

Or do you not know that the unrighteous will not inherit the kingdom of God? Do not be deceived: none of these will enter the kingdom of God:

- Sexually immoral
- Idolaters
- Adulterers
- Homosexuality
- Thieves
- the Greedy
- Drunkards
- Revilers
- Swindlers

<u>**1 Corinthians 11:29-30**</u>

For he who eats and drinks in an unworthy manner eats and drinks judgment to himself, not discerning the Lord's body. For this reason many are weak and sick among you, and many sleep.

- Taking communion in an unworthy manner

<u>**2 Corinthians 4:2**</u>

But we have renounced the hidden things of shame, not walking in craftiness nor handling the word of God deceitfully, but by manifestation of the truth commending ourselves to every man's conscience in the sight of God.

- Hiding shame
- Walking in craftiness
- Deceitfully handling God's word

<u>**2 Corinthians 11:12-15**</u>

But what I do, I will also continue to do, that I may cut off the opportunity from those who desire an opportunity to be regarded just as we are in the things of which they boast. For such are false apostles, deceitful workers, transforming themselves into apostles of Christ. And no wonder! For Satan himself transforms himself into an angel of light. Therefore it is no great thing if his ministers also transform themselves into ministers of righteousness, whose end will be according to their work

- False apostles of Christ

<u>**2 Corinthians 12:20-21**</u>

For I fear lest, when I come, I shall not find you such as I wish, and that I shall be found by you such as you do not wish; lest there be:

- Contentiousness
- Jealousies
- Outbursts of wrath
- Selfish ambitions
- Backbitings
- Whisperings
- Conceits
- Tumults
- Uncleanness
- Fornication
- Lewdness

<u>**Galatians 5:19-21**</u>

Now the works of the flesh are evident. I warn you, as I warned you before, that those who do such things will not inherit the kingdom of God:

- Envy
- Drunkenness
- Orgies
- Sexual immorality
- Impurity
- Sensuality
- Idolatry
- Sorcery
- Enmity
- Strife
- Jealousy
- Fits of anger

- Rivalries
- Dissensions
- Divisions
- Envy
- Drunkenness
- Orgies

Ephesians 4:26-27

Be angry, and do not sin": do not let the sun go down on your wrath, nor give place to the devil.

- Prolonged anger
- Giving place to the devil

Ephesians 4:31

Let all bitterness, wrath, anger, clamor, and evil speaking be put away from you, with all malice.

- Bitterness
- Wrath
- Anger
- Clamor
- Evil speaking with malice

Ephesians 5:3-5

But fornication and all uncleanness or covetousness, let it not even be named among you, as is fitting for saints; neither filthiness, nor foolish talking, nor coarse jesting, which are not fitting, but rather giving of thanks. For this you know, that no fornicator, unclean person, nor covetous man, who is an idolater, has any inheritance in the kingdom of Christ and God.

- Filthiness (uncleanness)

- Foolish talking
- Coarse jesting
- Fornication
- Covetousness
- Idolatry

Ephesians 6:4

And you, fathers, do not provoke your children to wrath, but bring them up in the training and admonition of the Lord.

- Provoking children to wrath

Philippians 2:13-25

Do all things without complaining and disputing, hat you may become blameless and harmless, children of God without fault in the midst of a crooked and perverse generation, among whom you shine as lights in the world.

- Grumbling & complaining

Philippians 3:18-19; James 4:4; 1 John 2:15-17

For many walk, of whom I have told you often, and now tell you even weeping, that they are the enemies of the cross of Christ: whose end is destruction, whose god is their belly, and whose glory is in their shame— who set their mind on earthly things. Do you not know that friendship with the world is enmity with God? Whoever therefore wants to be a friend of the world makes himself an enemy of God. Do not love the world or the things in the world. If anyone loves the world, the love of the Father is not in him. For all that is in the world—the lust of the flesh, the lust of the eyes, and the pride of life—is not of the Father but is of the world. And the world is passing away, and the lust of it; but he who does the will of God abides forever.

- Love the World – Lust of the flesh

- Love the World – Lust of the eyes
- Love the World – Pride of life

Colossians 3:4-10

When Christ who is your life appears, then you also will appear with him in glory. Put to death therefore what is earthly in you:

- Sexual immorality
- Impurity
- Passion
- Evil desire
- Covetousness which is idolatry
- Anger
- Wrath
- Malice
- Slander
- Obscene talk from your mouth

1 Timothy 1:8-11

Now we know that the law is good, if one uses it lawfully, understanding this, that the law is not laid down for the just but for the lawless and disobedient, for the ungodly and sinners, for the unholy and profane and whatever else is contrary to sound doctrine, in accordance with the gospel of the glory of the blessed God with which I have been entrusted:

- Those who strike their parents
- Murderers
- Sexually immoral
- Homosexuals
- Enslavers
- Liars
- Perjurers

1 Timothy 1:12-13

And I thank Christ Jesus our Lord who has enabled me, because He counted me faithful, putting me into the ministry, although I was formerly a blasphemer, a persecutor, and an insolent man; but I obtained mercy because I did it ignorantly in unbelief.

- Blaspheming
- Persecuting
- Insolence

1 Timothy 2:9; Proverbs 7:10

...that the women adorn themselves in modest apparel, with propriety and moderation... And there a woman met him, with the attire of a harlot, and a crafty heart.

- Dress provocatively

1 Timothy 3:6; James 4:6

lest being puffed up with pride he fall into the same condemnation as the devil.... God resists the proud, But gives grace to the humble.

- Pride

1 Timothy 4:1-3

Now the Spirit expressly says that in latter times some will depart from the faith, giving heed to deceiving spirits and doctrines of demons, speaking lies in hypocrisy, having their own conscience seared with a hot iron, forbidding to marry, and commanding to abstain from foods which God created to be received with thanksgiving.

- Giving heed to doctrines of demons
- Hypocrisy

1 Timothy 5:13

And besides they learn to be idle, wandering about from house to house, and not only idle but also gossips and busybodies, saying things which they ought not.

- Idleness
- Gossips
- Busybodies

1 Timothy 6:10

For the love of money is a root of all kinds of evil, for which some have strayed from the faith in their greediness, and pierced themselves through with many sorrow.

- Love of money

2 Timothy 2:16

But shun profane and idle babblings, for they will increase to more ungodliness.

- Vain babblings

2 Timothy 3:1–5

But understand this, that in the last days there will come times of difficulty, for people will be sinful. Avoid such people:

- Lovers of self
- Lovers of money
- Proud
- Arrogant
- Abusive
- Disobedient to their parents

- Ungrateful
- Unholy
- Heartless
- Unappeasable
- Slanderous
- Without self-control
- Brutal
- Not loving good
- Treacherous
- Reckless
- Swollen with conceit
- Lovers of pleasure rather than God
- A form of godliness without power

2 Timothy 4:4

and they will turn their ears away from the truth, and be turned aside to fable

- Preferring fables over truth

Titus 3:3

For we ourselves were once:

- Foolish
- Disobedient
- Led astray
- Slaves to various passions and pleasures
- Passing our days in malice and envy
- Hating one another

James 2:1-5

My brethren, do not hold the faith of our Lord Jesus Christ, the Lord of glory, with partiality. For if there should come into your assembly a man

*with gold rings, in fine apparel, and there should also come in a poor man
in filthy clothes, and you pay attention to the one wearing the fine clothes
and say to him, "You sit here in a good place," and say to the poor man,
"You stand there," or, "Sit here at my footstool," have you not [1]shown
partiality among yourselves, and become judges with evil thoughts?
Listen, my beloved brethren: Has God not chosen the poor of this world to
be rich in faith and heirs of the kingdom which He promised to those who
love Him?*

- Partiality

James 3:14-15
*But if you have bitter envy and self-seeking in your hearts, do not boast
and lie against the truth. This wisdom does not descend from above, but is
earthly, sensual, demonic.*

- bitter envy
- self-seeking in your hearts
- boasting
- lying

James 4:16
But now you boast in your arrogance. All such boasting is evil.

- Arrogant boasting

James 4:17
Therefore, to him who knows to do good and does not do it, to him it is sin.

- Knowing the right thing to do and not doing it

James 5:4; 1 Thessalonians 4:6

Indeed the wages of the laborers who mowed your fields, which you kept back by fraud, cry out; and the cries of the reapers have reached the ears of the Lord of Sabaoth... that no one should take advantage of and defraud his brother in this matter, because the Lord is the avenger of all such, as we also forewarned you and testified.

- Withholding wages earned

1 Peter 2:1-3

Therefore, laying aside all malice, all deceit, hypocrisy, envy, and all evil speaking, as newborn babes, desire the pure milk of the word, that you may grow thereby, if indeed you have tasted that the Lord is gracious.

- Malice
- Deceit
- Hypocrisy
- Envy
- Evil speaking

1 Peter 3:9

not returning evil for evil or reviling for reviling, but on the contrary blessing, knowing that you were called to this, that you may inherit a blessing.

- Returning insult for insult

2 Peter 2:10

and especially those who walk according to the flesh in the lust of uncleanness and despise authority. They are presumptuous, self-willed. They are not afraid to speak evil of dignitaries

- Presumptuous and self-willed

2 Peter 3:3

knowing this first: that scoffers will come in the last days, walking according to their own lust

- Scoffers

2 Peter 3:16; Galatians 1:7-8

as also in all his epistles, speaking in them of these things, in which are some things hard to understand, which untaught and unstable people twist to their own destruction, as they do also the rest of the Scriptures.... but there are some who trouble you and want to pervert the gospel of Christ. But even if we, or an angel from heaven, preach any other gospel to you than what we have preached to you, let him be accursed.

- Twisting the Word of God

1 John 2:15; James 4:4-7; Philippians 3:18-19

For many walk, of whom I have told you often, and now tell you even weeping, that they are the enemies of the cross of Christ: whose end is destruction, whose god is their belly, and whose glory is in their shame—who set their mind on earthly things.... Do you not know that friendship with the world is enmity with God? Whoever therefore wants to be a friend of the world makes himself an enemy of God.... Do not love the world or the things in the world. If anyone loves the world, the love of the Father is not in him.

- Love of the world

1 John 3:4

Everyone who makes a practice of sinning also practices lawlessness; sin is:

- Lawlessness

1 John 2:11; 4:20; Titus 3:3

But he who hates his brother is in darkness and walks in darkness, and does not know where he is going, because the darkness has blinded his eyes. If someone says, "I love God," and hates his brother, he is a liar; for he who does not love his brother whom he has seen, how can he love God whom he has not seen? [They are] living in malice and envy, hateful and hating one another.

- Hating one another

1 John 3:17

But whoever has this world's goods, and sees his brother in need, and shuts up his heart from him, how does the love of God abide in him?

- Not giving to the needy

1 John 3:23

And this is His commandment: that we should believe on the name of His Son Jesus Christ and love one another, as He gave us commandment.

- Unbelief in the name of Jesus Christ

1 John 5:16-17

If anyone sees his brother committing a sin not leading to death, he shall ask, and God will give him life—to those who commit sins that do not lead to death. I do not say that one should pray for that. All wrongdoing is sin, but there is:

- Sin that leads to death
- Sin that does not lead to death

Jude 16-19

These are grumblers, complainers, walking according to their own lusts; and they mouth great swelling words, flattering people to gain advantage. But you, beloved, remember the words which were spoken before by the apostles of our Lord Jesus Christ: how they told you that there would be mockers in the last time who would walk according to their own ungodly lusts. These are sensual persons, who cause divisions, not having the Spirit.

- Grumblers
- Complainers
- Flatterers
- Mockers
- Sensual persons
- Cause divisions

Revelation 3:15-16

"I know your works, that you are neither cold nor hot. I could wish you were cold or hot. So then, because you are lukewarm, and neither cold nor hot, I will vomit you out of My mouth"

- Lukewarm Christianity

Revelation 9:21

And they did not repent of their murders or their sorceries [drugs] or their sexual immorality or their thefts.

- Murder
- Sorceries [drugs]
- Sexual immorality
- Thefts

Revelation 18:23

The light of a lamp shall not shine in you anymore, and the voice of bridegroom and bride shall not be heard in you anymore. For your merchants were the great men of the earth, for by your sorcery all the nations were deceived.

- Sorcery

Revelation 21:8

But as for these, their portion will be in the lake that burns with fire and sulfur, which is the second death:

- Cowardly
- Faithless
- Detestable
- Murderers
- Sexually immoral
- Sorcerers
- Idolaters
- Liars

Revelation 22:15

But outside are dogs and sorcerers and sexually immoral and murderers and idolaters, and whoever loves and practices a lie.

- Sorcerers
- Sexually immoral
- Idolaters
- Liars

Revelation 22:18–19

For I testify to everyone who hears the words of the prophecy of this book: If anyone adds to these things, God will add to him the plagues that are written in this book; and if anyone takes away from the words of the book of this prophecy, God shall take away his part from the Book of Life, from the holy city, and from the things which are written in this book.

- Adding or subtracting from God's word

It is no wonder that "all have sinned." As you can see, this is a bottomless list and the sincere soul will never be free from the law as the Pauline scriptures explain. We may take, for example, the instruction on divorce beginning with the Malachi expression that "God hates divorce." Was he talking about Israel's harlotry with foreign gods or was Malachi focused on the legality of divorce between a man and woman? Jesus' own explanation, when the Pharisees tried to trap him in a technicality, was that Moses allowed it only because of the Israelites' hardness of heart, and that "what God joined (in marriage), no man should put asunder." Now we are left with the question, "Did God join us, or did we leave Him out of the decision?" Was there adultery or allowance given by Jesus for this divorce? Since Jesus did not mention extreme abuse, can that be used as a reason? Regretfully we find ourselves in legalism, unsure of our sin. What Christian man can say that he has never looked on a woman with lust in his heart? Men are very, very visual in their sexual desire. Granted we don't go around wishing we could have sex with that woman or another, but when does appreciation for beauty become lust? Again, we are trapped in legalism. Admittedly, some Scripture is not so easy for us to come to terms with, e.g. John's comment that he does not say that we should pray for a person committing a sin leading to death. But, doesn't all sin lead to death? Or, we might ask, when does my provision of constructive criticism become the sin of grumbling? What constitutes "loving the world? When does my love for conversation become "vain babblings?" What's the difference between righteous indignation and anger that God would not allow? What exactly constitutes adding to or subtracting from God's word? Does God choose that we be like Muslims who must "walk on the razor's edge," not knowing for sure when we might be sinning or not? There must then be a better way that goes to first principles. It is there that Part II, The Sin Principle attempts to take us.

This Is Thy Will I Know

Charles Wesley – 1749

This is Thy will I know -
That I should holy be,
Should let my sins this moment go,
This moment turn to Thee.
O, might I now embrace
Thy all sufficient pow'r,
And Never more to sin give place,
And never grieve Thee more!

I Lay My Sins On Jesus

Horatius Bonar – 1843

I lay my sins on Jesus,
The spotless Lamb of God;
He bears them all, and frees us
From the accursed load.
I bring my guilt to Jesus,
To wash my crimson stains
White in His blood most precious,,
Till not a spot remains.

CHAPTER 6
THE WRATH OF GOD
(His Terrifying Warning)[9]

"God gave them over to uncleanness, vile passions, and a debased mind." – Paul

Lest my reader think the author is angry and "unloving" in daring to broach this subject, let me assure him that I find no pleasure in dwelling on God's wrath. It is clear that judgment belongs to Him. "Judge not lest you be judged," was Jesus' command for He understood that we cannot at the same time hate the sin and love the sinner. Habakkuk's concern was that God was allowing evil to thrive unchecked. God simply assured him that recompense was His and not man's, that He would work a work in the prophet's day, and that judgement would surely come and it would not tarry:

But the Lord is in His holy temple. Let all the earth keep silence before Him (Hab 2:20).

Is God qualified to judge? A Psalm of David reminds us that *the earth is the Lord's, and all its fullness, the world and those who dwell therein, for He has founded it upon the seas, and established it upon the waters* (Psa 24:1-2). *Know that the Lord, He is God; it is he who has made us, and not we ourselves; we are His people and the sheep of his pasture* (Psa 100:3). *God shows no partiality* (Acts 10:34). And there is no creature hidden from His sight, but all things are naked and open to the eyes of Him to whom we must give an account (Heb 4:13). Has He placed on us too great a burden? The Apostle John didn't think so (1 John 5:2-4). Jesus, Himself, said that His yoke was easy and

His burden was light (Matt 11:30). As the gospel song says, "I've found it so; I've found it so." Is His justice fair? The song of Moses (Deut 32:4) puts it this way:

He is the Rock, his work is perfect; For all His ways are justice, A God of truth and without injustice; Righteous and upright is He. The reality is that God is a just judge, and God is angry with the wicked every day (Psa 7:11)

Jesus said, we don't have to fear those who kill the body; we need to fear the one who has the authority to cast us into hell. "Yes, I tell you, fear Him" said Jesus (Luke 12:1-5). He is the God of love, but He is also the God who will judge us. We need not fear evil, for God is with us and will guard our hearts. We need not fear the terror of the night, nor the arrow that flies by day, not the pestilence that stalks in darkness, not the destruction that wastes at noonday, because we dwell in the shelter of the most high (Psa 91:1-6). The same Christ who died for us will say, "Depart from Me, I never knew you" (Matt 7:23). The Great White Throne Judgment of Revelation 20:11-15 pictures those who are not found written in the Book of Life. Those not found saved by grace and faith in Jesus Christ will be "cast into the lake of fire." How can a loving God send people to an eternal hell? The question is difficult to answer, but the Scripture says that it will be so.

For who has known the mind of the Lord? Or who has become His counselor? Or who has first given to Him and it shall be repaid to him? (Rom 11:34-35 quoting Job 36:22 and Job 41:11)

Modern man believes that he will know the difference between right and wrong without God's help, but he fails to know it. There is a wide gap between the wisest non-believer and children of faith, and even between the redeemed Christian and the consecrated Christian. John the Baptist captured the difference in his harvesting metaphor:

I indeed baptize you with water unto repentance, but He who is coming after me is mightier than I, whose sandals I am not worthy to carry. He will baptize you with the Holy Spirit and fire. His winnowing fan is in His hand, and he will thoroughly clean out His threshing floor, and gather His wheat into the barn; but He will burn up the chaff with unquenchable fire (Matt 3:11–12).

God intends us to be clean, to be separated unto holiness. When He does this work in us, He also exonerates us from judgment, rescues us from death and darkness and introduces us to light and life. He seals us from Satan and into Himself. He is ours and we are His. While we do not deserve this privilege and treatment, this mercy and grace, this new life everlasting, we receive it because we value His cross. For it is His blood that covers our sins never to be remembered against us again.

There is therefore now no condemnation to them which are in Christ Jesus (Rom 8:1).

After considering the horror of God's judgment, we must leave it up to Him, for we cannot bear the thought of it. Hell is described in terms of fire and brimstone, outer darkness, wailing and gnashing of teeth, but it may also be defined as eternal separation from God. This warning is scattered throughout Scripture. We know that He loves us, but we must remember that He is also our judge. Has our judge shown mercy toward us? Oh, you know that He has!

The Garden of Eden represents to us not only a beautiful place of innocence but a place of fulfillment and purpose. The Bible describes the Lord as walking in the garden in the cool of the day. Having sinned Adam and Eve tried to hide themselves from the presence of the Lord. Normally, they would not have been afraid or had a need to hide. They had been enjoying the "presence of the Lord!" God confronted them because of their disobedience. The cost was great. They were not only banished from the garden, but life became difficult and full of toil and pain. God allowed their sorrow to be greatly multiplied. The very ground they walked on was allowed to be cursed so that they had to struggle for survival. In the garden they coexisted with "the Tree of Life," but now God told them that they would return to the ground from which they were taken. The Bible teaches that the sin of Adam and Eve is passed along to Cain and Abel and to every offspring including us. We come into this world completely selfish with the tendency to sin, already out of fellowship with God. That puts us all under the same sentence of death.

After generations had passed, God looked on mankind, saw his wickedness, that he was only evil continually. The Bible says that God was grieved in His heart and sorry that He had made man on the earth. So He said, "I will destroy man whom I have created from the face of the earth" (Gen 6:5–7). We should ask, why did Noah "find grace in the eyes of the Lord?" It was because he was "a just man, perfect in his generations." He walked with God. (Gen 6:9).

It may be true that men don't learn simply from God's wrath. The Bible makes it clear that the heart of man is continually evil:

The heart is deceitful above all things, and desperately wicked; who can know it? I, the Lord, search the heart, I test the mind, even to give every man according to his ways, according to the fruit of his doings (Jer 17:9–10).

In Genesis 9:25 Noah observed that his grandson Canaan had the same sexual perversions as his father Ham. How long had God been waiting for the Canaanites to repent? How could God instruct Joshua to totally annihilate them upon entering the Promised Land? Is it that the Israelites were morally superior to the Canaanites that positioned them to cast the first stone? Without trying to mitigate or tone down the divine command to totally wipe out the population of Canaan, the text that places this whole question in perspective is Moses' explanation to Israel after their own rebellion:[10]

Do not think in your heart, after the Lord your God has cast them out before you, saying, 'Because of my righteousness the Lord has brought me in to possess this land'; but it is because of the wickedness of these nations that the Lord is driving them out from before you. It is not because of your righteousness or the uprightness of your heart that you go in to possess their land, but because of the wickedness of these nations that the Lord your God drives them out from before you, and that He may fulfill the word which the Lord swore to your fathers, to Abraham, Isaac, and Jacob. Therefore understand that the Lord your God is not giving you this good land to possess because of your righteousness, for you are a stiff-necked people (Deut 9:4–6).

God had told Abram, who at the time was in a deep sleep, and which Abram later described as a "horrible darkness" which fell on him, that his descendants would be enslaved in a foreign land for 400 years after which God would judge their oppressors. The children of Abram would come out with great possessions. Furthermore, God told him that his descendants in the fourth generation would return to the land He had promised him. Why did God delay this? God explained that the "iniquity of the Amorites" who occupied Canaan "was not yet complete" (Gen 15:12–16).

God does not pervert justice, but as judge of all the earth, he does what is right and at the right time. The issue here is the whole question of the legitimacy and meaning of divine anger. Too frequently men have tended to define anger as "the desire for retaliation," or the burning need to get even for some slight or actual harm that had been carried out against them. Some have even defined anger as a "brief madness," but in the context of divine anger it is best understood as "a motion of the soul rousing itself to curb sin." [11]

God's anger and wrath are His legitimate expressions of His abhorrence of all that is sinful, wrong, unjust, and against His very nature and being. This is not because sin damages God but because it damages His creatures and His creation. God did not flare up with an impetuosity against the Canaanites, but gave them centuries and millennia to get the point and right the wrong. In the end, He had to act or He would not be holy, just, righteous and fair.[12]

So rend your heart, and not your garments; return to the Lord your God, for He is gracious and merciful, slow to anger, and of great kindness; and he relents from doing harm (Joel 2:13).

Although God loves the man, He hates the sin and must act accordingly. That subject is skirted by many Christian preachers and teachers, for they do not want to offend the sensibilities of their audience. However, in the Old Testament there are more than twenty words in nearly six hundred key passages that deal with the topic of God's wrath. In the New Testament there are two main Greek words for wrath,' *thumos*' and '*orge*', both depicting a coming judgment that continues to mount up until finally God's patience can no longer justify His refraining from action.[13]

For the wrath of God is revealed from heaven against all ungodliness and unrighteousness of men, who suppress the truth in unrighteousness, because what may be known of God is manifest in them, for God has shown it to them (Rom 1:18–20).

God is angry because mortals have suppressed His own general revelation of Himself.   Despite this vast evidence in nature, men and women have refused to acknowledge it. As a result Paul goes on to explain in Romans, their minds have been darkened, their hearts have become foolish and substitutes for the true religion have been invented. So don't think that "religion" is the answer. It may be the evidence of the total depravity of mankind.

Woe to you, scribes and Pharisees, hypocrites! For you are like whitewashed tombs which indeed appear beautiful outwardly, but inside are full of dead men's bones and all uncleanness (Matt 23:27).

In general, the chief priests and Pharisees were threatened by Jesus' miracles of healing and the crowds that were following Him. They reasoned that the Romans would come and take away both their place and their nation. They plotted to put Him to death. Although He had done so many signs before them, they did not believe in Him. John reports that even among the rulers, many believed in Him, but because of the Pharisees they did not confess Him, lest they should be put out of the synagogue; for they loved the praise of men more than the praise of God. It is no wonder that Isaiah had prophesied 700 years before:

He has blinded their eyes and hardened their hearts, lest they should see with their eyes, lest they should understand with their hearts and turn, so that I should heal them (Isaiah 6:9–10).

Isaiah 6:9-10 reveals a terrifying warning, that God will actually harden hearts. It's as if God sees that they are never going to believe so He withdraws His mercy. He in a sense begins his judgment at that moment.

He came to His own and His own did not receive Him (John 1:11-13). Jesus told them, "If you had believed Moses, you would believe Me (John 5:46)." What a condemnation of the students of the Old Testament! He had cried out to the Jews *"He who believes in Me, believes not in Me but in Him who sent Me. And he who sees Me sees Him who sent Me. I have come as a light into the world, that whoever believes in Me should not abide in darkness. But if that person rejects Me, and does not receive My words, the very words I speak will judge him in the last day* (John 12:44-50).

Earlier John the Baptist had confronted the Pharisees and Sadducees by saying, *Brood of vipers! Who warned you to flee from the wrath to come? Therefore bear fruits worthy of repentance, and do not think to say to yourselves, "We have Abraham as our father." For I say to you that God is able to raise up children to Abraham from these stones. And even now the ax is laid to the root of the trees. Therefore every tree which does not bear good fruit is cut down and thrown into the fire* (Matt 3:7-10). John the Baptist, the forerunner of Jesus Christ, had been preaching in the wilderness of Judea, saying "Repent, for the kingdom of heaven is at hand!" But to the religious leaders he said, "Who warned you?"

We have a little hope for the Pharisees. Nicodemus came to Jesus by night to enquire of Him. Saul, who described himself as a Pharisee of Pharisees, would later receive Jesus and become a great missionary for Christ. But the faithlessness of most of them was glaring. When the blind man said "I believe! and worshipped Jesus, Jesus said, "For judgment I have come into this world, that those who do not see may see, and that those who see may be made blind."

The Pharisees overheard and took offense: "Are we blind also?" Jesus replied, "If you were blind, you would have no sin; but now you say, "We see." Therefore your sin remains.

In Romans chapter 1 Paul reiterates three times that "God gave them over." He gave them over in the lusts of their hearts to impurity, He gave them over to degrading passions and He gave them over to a depraved mind. Why? They "exchanged the truth of God for a lie" (Rom 1:25).

Once again we see a pattern due to the downward spiral of sin: First God "gives them up in the lusts of their hearts to impurity." Then He "gives them up to the degrading of their bodies among themselves." Finally, He abandons them "to their own depraved minds" as they are filled with every kind of wickedness, evil, covetousness, malice, envy, murder, strife, deceit, craftiness, gossip, slander. In this they become God-haters, insolent, haughty, boastful, inventors of evil, rebellious toward parents, foolish, faithless, heartless, ruthless (Rom 1:24-32).

Paul in 2 Thessalonians chapter 2 speaks of the coming "man of lawlessness" who will set himself up in the temple at some future time to be worshipped. He had explained to them before, so here he just tells them, "you know what restrains him now" (vs. 5). Various interpreters of this scripture say that the restrainer was Rome in Paul's time, or that it is the church, or that it is the Holy Spirit. Perhaps, it is the angel Michael. The Bible does not tell us here. Paul goes on to describe the "deception of wickedness for those who perish, because they did not receive the love of the truth so as to be saved. Then come verses 11 &12:

> *And for this reason God will send upon them a deluding influence so that they might believe what is false, in order that they all may be judged who did not believe the truth, but took pleasure in wickedness* (2 Thes 2:11-12).

"Soon will pass God's day of grace" says the song we have printed at the end of this chapter. One example can be found in 2 Chron 36:15–16. Young King Zedekiah did evil in the sight of the Lord his God and did not humble himself when spoken to by the prophet Jeremiah. "God sent word to them again and again by His messengers, because He had compassion on his people and on His dwelling place; but they continually mocked the messengers of God, despised God's words and scoffed at His prophets, until the wrath of the Lord arose against His people, until there was no remedy."

Therefore He brought against them the king of the Chaldeans, who killed their young men with the sword in the house of their sanctuary, and had no compassion on young man or virgin, on the aged or the weak; He gave them all into his hand. And all the articles from the house of God, great and small, the treasures of the house of the Lord, and the treasures of the king and of his leaders, all these he took to Babylon. Then they burned the house of God, broke down the wall of Jerusalem, burned all its palaces with fire, and destroyed all its precious possessions. And those who escaped from the sword he carried away to Babylon, where they became servants to him and his sons until the rule of the kingdom of Persia, to fulfill the word of the Lord by the mouth of Jeremiah (2 Chron 36:17–21).

Isaiah had earlier urged Israel:

Seek the Lord while He may be found; Call upon Him while He is near. Let the wicked forsake his way, And the unrighteous man his thoughts; And let him return to the Lord, And He will have compassion on him; And to our God, For He will abundantly pardon (Isa 55:6–7).

It is true that the Lord is gracious and merciful, slow to anger and great in lovingkindness (Psa 145:8), but it is also true that "He will not always strive with us, nor will He keep His anger forever" (Psa 103:9).

HAVE YOU ANY ROOM FOR JESUS?
(anonymous)

1. Have you any room for Jesus,
   He who bore your load of sin?
   As He knocks and asks admission,
   Sinner, will you let Him in?

2. Room for pleasure, room for business –
   But for Christ, the Crucified,
   Not a place that He can enter
   In the heart for which He died?

3. Have you any room for Jesus,
   As in grace He calls again?
   O today is time accepted;
   Later you may call in vain.

4. Room and time now give to Jesus;
   Soon will pass God's day of grace –
   Soon your heart left cold and silent,
   And your Savior's pleading cease.

Ch–Room for Jesus, King of Glory!
   Hasten now; His Word obey.
   Swing the heart's door widely open;
   Bid Him enter while you may.

PART II
THE SIN PRINCIPLE

CHAPTER 7
THE BLAME GAME (Original Sin)

"Sin is my claim to my right to myself."
– Oswald Chambers

What is the motivation for sin? What are the causal roots within the nature of the unsanctified man? The Bible uses several phrases which carry the doctrine of original sin: inherited depravity, Adamic sin, inherent depravity, inbred sin, indwelling sin, the law of sin, the sinful nature, a worldly condition, and the flesh (contrasted with "the Spirit").

Inherited depravity, or that corruption of moral nature passed down to a man through his birth, is not destroyed at conversion, or cleansed away in regeneration. It is mastered, conquered, but not annihilated.[14] The doctrine of "Adamic depravity" is thoroughly taught by scripture. One cannot ignore it. Adam and Eve were created "in the image of God" (Gen 5:1-2). When Adam had a son, that son was "in <u>his</u> own likeness, in <u>his</u> own image (Gen 5:3). Since the fall of Adam we are told that "every inclination of man's heart is evil from childhood" (Gen 8:21).

Although children are innocent in their sin, having not yet attained adult accountability, there is no mistaking the inherent selfishness of a child. His most frequently used words are "I, my, me & mine."

God does not punish children for original sin (Matt 18:3; Mark 10:14; Deut 1:39), but the nature to sin common to every man ever born after Adam & Eve, is to act out what is already there in the heart. For adults that is sin, and God will hold us accountable. Why do we believe this? We believe the unregenerate are free to do a righteous act only when helped by prevenient grace.

The Bible tells us that "in Adam, all die." But it also tells us "in Christ all shall be made alive" (1 Cor 15:22).

Some Difficulties With the Doctrine of "original sin:"

- It seems unfair. This would be so were it not for Christ's "undoing" of the dilemma.

- Unavoidable guilt is nearly an oxymoron. How can we be guilty of something someone else has done? The answer is that Adam was our representative. Although we are not guilty of Adam's specific sin, we do carry within us "Adamic depravity," the tendency to sin.

Some theological words for this condition of the human heart are: **Original Sin** referring to the state we are in due to that original act of sin on Adam's part, **Inherited Depravity** which may mislead some into thinking it is based on the sins of their parents, **Adamic Sin** which means that because of Adam's fall we are given a bias toward acts of sin, **Inherent Depravity** which unfortunately may imply that there is no redemption, **Inbred Sin** which may sound like sin is bred into our genes such that we cannot change, **Racial Depravity** which reminds us that this tendency to sin is shared by the entire human race, and **Adamic Depravity** which traces the origin to the fall of the human race.

But how is this Adamic depravity transmitted? Some believe that we were somehow racially bound up with and in Adam to such extent that we actually sinned when he did. This is the theory of Augustine and of many theologians in the Calvinistic tradition.

Others believe we each come into the world in a state of sinfulness because Adam had been chosen as our representative and because our representative sinned against God. This is sometimes called the "Federalist Theory." This may at first seem a distinction without a difference. Do we carry the sin gene in our DNA or RNA? That's a possibility but not necessary to the federalist theory of transmission. It is enough to say that the propensity or inclination to acts of sin originated with Adam and is unavoidable except by the virgin birth of Jesus.

We speak of sin, first of all, in the generic sense. If "adamic nature" be the primary root, several "rootlets" stem from this nature. The next four chapters speak of these separately so that we realize the forms original sin can take.

It Is Well with My Soul
Spafford, 1873 & Bliss, 1876

My sin – O the bliss of this glorious tho't –
My sin – not in part, but the whole –
Is nailed to the cross, and I bear it no more!
Praise the Lord, praise the Lord, O my soul!

CHAPTER 8
IGNORANCE (Sin Principle 1)

For as I was passing through and considering the objects of your worship, I even found an altar with this inscription: TO THE UNKNOWN GOD. Therefore, the One whom you worship without knowing, Him I proclaim to you (Acts 17:23)

How then shall they call on Him in whom they have not believed? And how shall they believe in Him of whom they have not heard? And how shall they hear without a preacher? (Rom 10:14)

If I had not come and spoken to them, they would have no sin, but now they have no excuse for their sin (John 15:22).

Although God does not hold us accountable for what we do not know, it is clear that as "children of the Creator" we must be taught the difference between right and wrong in order to avoid sin. In Acts 17:23 Paul confronted a people worshipping an unknown god. The Bible makes it clear that man must be told of his sin in order to keep from sinning. We are responsible for what we know. But we cannot feign ignorance once God has spoken to us.

Nevertheless I tell you the truth. It is to your advantage that I go away; for if I do not go away, the Helper will not come to you; but if I depart, I will send Him to you. And when He has come, He will convict the world of sin, and of righteousness, and of judgment: of sin, because they do not believe in Me; of righteousness, because I go to My Father

When we refuse to listen to God or believe Him, we sin against Him, since He has no deficiency in His ability to communicate effectively. He does not lie and is completely trustworthy. The conviction by the Holy Spirit should lead a man to confess this sin and repent.

The lowly shepherds listened to the angels, went and saw Jesus, and made widely known the saying which was told them by the angels. They glorified and praised God for all the things they had heard and seen. They were no longer ignorant of the Savior for all whom would believe.

Sweet Little Jesus Boy

Robert MacGimsey, 1934

Sweet little Jesus boy
They made you be born in a manger
Sweet little holy child
Didn't know who you was
Didn't know you'd come to save us Lord
To take our sins away
Our eyes were blind, we could not see
Didn't know who you was

CHAPTER 9
UNBELIEF (Sin Principle 2)

There could be no more acceptable faith to God than this, which takes God at His word, and goes on without a disturbing doubt. – Beverly Carradine -1890

Unbelief and doubt are the root of unlawfulness and faithlessness. The apostles preached that if you confess with your mouth the Lord Jesus and believe in your heart that God raised Him from the dead, you will be saved. With the heart one believes unto righteousness, and with the mouth confession is made unto salvation (Rom 10:9-10). The ultimate importance of believing in Christ is the salvation of the soul. To deny Christ's deity is to deny the salvation He came to earth to provide for sinful humanity. To accept it, is to have salvation.

> *But in accordance with your hardness and your impenitent heart you are treasuring up for yourself wrath in the day of wrath and revelation of the righteous judgment of God (Rom 2:5).*

The New Testament often ties unbelief to Jesus' willingness to heal and uplift.

> *Now He could do no mighty work there, except that He laid His hands on a few sick people and healed them. And He marveled because of their unbelief (Mark 6:5-6).*

> *Jesus said to him, "If you can believe, all things are possible to him who believes" Immediately the father of the child cried out and said with tears, "Lord, I believe; help my unbelief!" (Mark 9:23-24)*

Jesus said to her, "I am the resurrection and the life. He who believes in Me, though he may die, he shall live. And whoever lives and believes in Me shall never die. Do you believe this?" (Mark 11:25-26)

He said to the ruler of the synagogue, Do not be afraid; only believe."... Immediately the girl arose and walked, for she was twelve years of age. And they were overcome with great amazement (Mark 5:36,42).

On the last day, the climax of the festival, Jesus stood and shouted to the crowds, "Anyone who is thirsty may come to me! Anyone who believes in me may come and drink! For the Scriptures declare, 'Rivers of living water will flow from his heart.'" (John 7:37-38)

I told you that you would die in your sins, for unless you believe that I am he you will die in your sins."... He who rejects Me, and does not receive My words, has that which judges him—the word that I have spoken will judge him in the last day (John 8:24; 12:48).

Unbelief leads to guilt and hopelessness. The conviction of the Holy Spirit should lead a man to confess this sin and repent. That leads to wonderful freedom and hope.

It's Real

Homer L. Cox, 1907

O how well do I remember how I doubted day by day
For I did not know for certain that my sins were washed away
When the spirit tried to tell me, I would not the truth receive;
I endeavored to be happy and to make myself believe.

CHAPTER 10
DISOBEDIENCE (Sin Principle 3)

So when the woman saw that the tree was good for food, that it was pleasant to the eyes, and a tree desirable to make one wise, she took of its fruit and ate. She also gave to her husband with her, and he ate (Gen 3:6).

Now by this we know that we know Him, if we keep His commandments. He who says, "I know Him," and does not keep His commandments, is a liar, and the truth is not in him. But whoever keeps His word, truly the love of God is perfected in him. By this we know that we are in Him. He who says he abides in Him ought himself also to walk just as He walked (1 John 2:3-6).

Disobedience is the willful disregard for a known commandment of God. Nowhere in the Scripture is it taught that there is "a law of necessity" with regard to sin, that sin entered human life as a matter of necessity, that it is inevitable and cannot be avoided. Neither does the Bible teach that sin was a natural limitation created within mankind. When we take this view we make a holy God the author of sin.

Adam and Eve were created (in the image of God) without sin; they were "very good" (Gen 1:31). God normally walked and talked with them (Gen 3:8). But fellowship was broken when the pair ate of the forbidden fruit, the single prohibition God had given them. As we have said earlier: There are three characteristics surrounding sin, 1) God gives a command, 2) God gives a warning and consequence, and 3) We are given a choice to obey or disobey. The misuse of free will to throw off restraint and to challenge God's authority are at the heart of this original sin.

A great example in Genesis of God's warning is when he saw hatred in Cain's heart. God said that sin lies at the door and you will have to rule over it. He did not rule over it and murdered Abel. God banished him from all the rest. His punishment, said Cain, was too much to bear (Gen 4:13).

Just as with the first family, God is faithful to give us commandments and to give us warning. I believe that God is so very glad when we decide to listen and obey, for He is not willing that any should perish. Because our obedience is never coerced, we can see that God desires that we choose to obey. Adam and Eve "walked with God in the cool of the day" before the fall. God would restore that love relationship. *"For this is the love of God, that we keep His commandments. And His commandments are not burdensome. For whatever is born of God overcomes the world. And this is the victory that has overcome the world—our faith"* (1 John 5:3-4).

Trust and Obey

Sammis & Towner, 1887

But we never can prove the delights of His love
Until all on the altar we lay;
For the favor He shows and the joy He bestows
Are for them who will trust and obey.

CHAPTER 11
REBELLION (Sin Principle 4)

Rebellion is the root of the desire for the forbidden. It leads to separation from God and it leads to death. But the good news is that God has provided atonement, justice and mercy through Christ's own blood on the cross. How wonderful to be forgiven and to respond in thankful obedience to such salvation! When we do a thing that we know is wrong simply because we want to do it, as with the drinking party of 1 Peter 4:3 or any such act, we are simply being rebellious. God does not ignore these things any more than any good parent who would raise a child of good character. God has set up moral restraints within which our free will can legitimately function. When we go outside of these "parental" boundaries, we know that we have done something wrong. Outside of God's boundaries lurk every sort of danger and enticement.

> *Woe to the rebellious children," says the LORD, "Who take counsel, but not of Me, And who devise plans, but not of My Spirit, That they may add sin to sin (Isa 30:1).*

This rebellion is characterized by a hardness of heart that will not listen to the God who loves you. This unruly behavior tends to spring up quite easily within human nature, regardless of age. It causes you to feel extremely rushed and driven, paranoid, angry, and prone to satisfy the flesh in the most expedient way. One of the worst things a person can do is harden their heart toward God. The consequences of such obstinacy are devastating. This is why the author of Hebrews wrote, "Today, if you hear His voice, do not harden your hearts as you did in the rebellion" (Hebrews 3:15).

The root is immaturity and unruliness. Rebellion leads to dissipation and misery of every kind. There is a great need for discipline and the guidance of God by the Holy Spirit. A man's response and repentance from rebellion lead to productivity and spiritual fruit. If this root is not overcome, sin will flow unabated.

At Calvary

Newell & Towner, 1895

Years I spent in vanity and pride,
Caring not my Lord was crucified,
Knowing not it was for me He died
On Calvary
By God's Word at last my sin I learned;
Then I trembled at the law I'd spurned,
Till my guilty soul imploring turned
To Calvary
Mercy there was great and grace was free;
Pardon there was multiplied to me;
There my burdened soul found liberty,
At Calvary.

CHAPTER 12

PERVERSION (Sin Principle 5)

Perversion is taking that which is holy and good and twisting it into something bad, ugly, belittling, crude and filthy, and making it into something for which God did not intend. When the money-changers made "the house of prayer into a den of thieves" (Matt 21:13), it was a perversion of God's purpose for the temple. There is no end of ways to pervert what is good just for the sake of doing it. This meanness, often couched in ungodly humor, springs from the desire to pull things down to sin's level. God has given the good, the pure, the beautiful, and the holy. We are to keep them so.

> *"Remember the Sabbath day, to keep it holy. Six days you shall labor and do all your work, but the seventh day is the Sabbath of the LORD your God. In it you shall do no work: you, nor your son, nor your daughter, nor your male servant, nor your female servant, nor your cattle, nor your stranger who is within your gates (Exod 20:8-10).*

> *Whatever things are true, whatever things are noble, whatever things are just, whatever things are pure, whatever things are lovely, whatever things are of good report, if there is any virtue and if there is anything praiseworthy—meditate on these things (Phil 4:8).*

> *For even their women exchanged the natural use for what is against nature. Likewise also the men, leaving the natural use of the woman, burned in their lust for one another, men with men committing what is shameful, and*

receiving in themselves the penalty of their error which was due (Rom 1:27).

And a voice spoke to him again the second time, "What God has cleansed you must not call common" (Acts 10:15).

This unholy warring against God only brings weakness and loss of health and sanity to a man. Only God's light brings a solution to such darkness! When a man responds to this light by consecrating himself wholly and completely by the cleansing of the Holy Spirit, there results an intimacy with God, power for ministry, holiness, and a heart for God. God remains our reference point and our measure for what is right and good (1 Pet 1:15-16). When a man perverts the truth and distorts the purposes of God, he is in danger of judgment:

But there shall by no means enter it anything that defiles, or causes an abomination or a lie, but only those who are written in the Lamb's Book of Life (Rev 21:27).

Is Thy Heart Right with God?
Elisha A. Hoffman (1839-1929)

Have thy affections been nailed to the cross?
Dost thou count all things for Jesus but loss?
Are all thy pow'rs under Jesus' control?
Does he each moment abide in thy soul?
Is thy heart right with God?
Washed in the crimson flood,
Cleansed and made holy, humble and lowly,
Right in the sight of God?

PART III
THE REMEDY

CHAPTER 13
CONVICTION OF SIN (God's Standard)

The unredeemed man who does not realize he is a sinner has no inclination toward God. Jeremiah 17:9 says, "*The heart is deceitful above all things, And desperately wicked; Who can know it?*" None of us could have known because his own sin must be discerned by the Spirit. The apostle Paul explained:

The natural man does not receive the things of the Spirit of God, for they are foolishness to him; nor can he know them, because they are spiritually discerned (1 Cor 2:14).

Jesus told His disciples this:

Nevertheless I tell you the truth. It is to your advantage that I go away; for if I do not go away, the Helper will not come to you; but if I depart, I will send Him to you. And when He has come, He will convict the world of sin, and of righteousness, and of judgment: of sin, because they do not believe in Me; of righteousness, because I go to My Father and you see Me no more (John 16:7–10).

Of fallen humans before conversion, Arminius writes: *In this state, the free will of man towards the true good is not only wounded, maimed, infirm, bent, and weakened; but it is also imprisoned, destroyed, and lost.*

And its powers are not only debilitated and useless unless they be assisted by grace, but it has no powers whatever except such as are excited by divine grace. For Christ has said, "Without me ye can do nothing, ...The mind, in this state, is dark, destitute of the saving knowledge of God, and, according to the Apostle, incapable of those things which belong to the Spirit of God.... Exactly correspondent to this darkness of the mind, and perverseness of the heart, is the utter weakness of all the powers to perform that which is truly good, and to omit the perpetration of that which is evil.[15]

J.I. Packer puts it this way: I am the slave of sin whom Christ must liberate; I am the fallen being who only have it in me to choose against God till God renews my heart.[16]

The heresy here we may call "humanism." This lie has been repeated often at graduations in forms such as William Ernest Henley's "Invictus" which ends with this line: "*I am the master of my fate; I am the captain of my soul.*" This philosophy will damn us for we are not able to free ourselves from sin. We must come to that place, by the conviction of the Holy Spirit, where we say "I am a sinner, and I need a Savior." Perhaps, your version might be "I am a victim and I need an emancipator." That philosophy will leave you open to every deception of men and demons, for the enemy of our souls is waiting and proficient in his lies and snares. He will promise to emancipate you, but he will only enslave you all the more.

What waits for you when God's Holy Spirit reveals your need? That is called "conviction," and brings us to a decision. Will I trust the convicting Holy Spirit or will I continue in my misery?

"God voted for me, the devil voted against me, and I
cast the deciding ballot for myself." – Bud Robinson

CHAPTER 14
GRACE (Mercy Applied)

We believe that there is a grace which seeks after us all. We call it "prevenient" because it comes before we know enough to ask. The Bible explains that there is nothing which is naturally within us to know that we are sinners, nothing within in us to believe there is any remedy for our misery and nothing that we would naturally seek outside of ourselves. In desperation we try to draw water from broken cisterns (Jer 2:13); we look in all the wrong places trying to satisfy the longings in our soul. We are like sheep who have gone astray, each to his own way. We would all be doing what seemed right in our own eyes. But grace presents a different story, a different reality. We can be changed. We are each and all sinners who need a Savior. There is such a Savior and He is reaching toward us to free us from sin and change us forever.

The Holy Spirit is the agent of prevenient grace who brings awareness of sin and opportunity to believe in the remedy of the cross of Christ. Oh, we cannot earn this at all; that is why we call it grace. There is nothing we can do to redeem ourselves. This is because we must trust Jesus for the gift of salvation. If there were a way to earn it or change ourselves through self-determinism and discipline, we would not have to trust in the only One who could ever lift us from sin and death. "God helps those who help themselves" is not in the Bible and not in the plan of God. We have found that the only way given is to trust in the Lord with all our heart and not to lean on our own understanding. The promise is not only that He will direct our paths, but that He will cleanse us from sin, give us a new life that is more abundant than we could have imagined, and place within in us an eternal hope.

Salvation is a big concept because although it has a beginning when we come to believe that Christ died for us, rose again, sits at the right hand of God where he intercedes for us, is coming again to judge the living and the dead, reward the faithful, create a new heaven and earth, reign for a thousand years, has prepared a place for us that we can be with Him, and so live evermore because of what Jesus did on the cross, we get a glimpse of eternity. All of this has come to us because of His grace and our response by faith.

> *For by grace have you been saved through faith, and*
> *that not of yourselves; it is the gift of God, not of works,*
> *lest any man should boast* (Eph 2:8-9).

Grace once received by me should be applied to others. That is why forgiveness is taught by Jesus in the Sermon on the Mount. I think Charles Swindoll's, The Grace Awakening (1990), is the best book he has written. It calls for us to apply God's antidote for prejudice and judgmental attitudes. It creates a desire to set people free from their yokes of slavery. We have a ministry of grace, which comes to us freely but cost the Savior His life.

That means we are free to believe on behalf of ourselves and others. We are free to minister without fear, knowing that He lives within us and can heal every broken heart, forgive every sin and set every captive free. We have the message of hope within us, and that is the energy of "grace awakened." Charles Swindoll points this out: "Most of us fall short when it comes to letting others be because of two strong very human tendencies: We compare ourselves with others (which leads us to criticize and compete with them) and we attempt to control others (which results in our manipulating or intimidating them.[17]

We tend to grossly under estimate the power of the cross to liberate us and others from the bondage and rule of sin in our lives.

Because of this, we undermine the Gospel. We pay attention to the whispers of Satan who would discourage and defeat. We live by fear rather than hope. We are defeated by the smallest of things. We assume that there are sins that cannot and should not be forgiven. We become cynical in our approach to those that we think have disqualified themselves due to wrong choices. We think that we ourselves are righteous because of good behavior and that we have done our share of good things even though that is not the message of the Scriptures. Christians should definitely experience an "emancipation proclamation." We need to realize the miracle of our own salvation, for we were not righteous, not one of us. We had turned away and become worthless; not one of us was good (Rom 3:10-12). However, when we chose to believe and receive the message of salvation, we were made clean by faith in Jesus. Having been set free by Jesus' own death on the cross, we are free indeed! (John 8:36). The Bible said He led captive a host of captives, even death itself. Knowing this grace, let us allow Him to keep all that would ruin us stay just that: captive!

His Grace Aboundeth More

Ulmer and Kirkpatrick, 1899

O what a wonderful Savior in Jesus, my Lord, I have found!
Tho' I had sins without number, His grace unto me did abound.
When a poor sinner he found me; no goodness to offer had I,
Often His law I had broken and merited naught but to die.
Nothing of merit possessing, all helpless before Him I lay;
But, in the precious blood flowing, He washed all my
        sin-stains away.
His grace aboundeth more. His grace aboundeth more.
Tho' sin abounded in my heart, His grace aboundeth more.

Wonderful Grace of Jesus

Haldor Lillenas, 1918

Wonderful grace of Jesus, greater than all my sin –
How shall my tongue describe it? Where shall His praise begin?
Taking away my burden, setting my spirit free;
For the wonderful grace of Jesus reaches me.
Wonderful grace of Jesus, reaching to all the lost –
By it I have been pardoned, saved to the uttermost.
Chains have been torn asunder, giving me liberty;
For the wonderful grace of Jesus reaches me.
Wonderful grace of Jesus, reaching the most defiled –
By its transforming power making him God's dear child,
Purchasing peace and heaven for all eternity;
And the wonderful grace of Jesus reaches me.
Wonderful the matchless grace of Jesus,
Deeper than the mighty rolling sea!
Higher than the mountain, sparkling like a fountain,
All sufficient grace for even me!
Broader than the scope of my transgressions,
Greater far than all my sin and shame!
O magnify the precious name of Jesus!
Praise His name!

CHAPTER 15

REDEMPTION (A Price to be Paid) [18]

...just as the Son of Man did not come to be served but to serve, and to give His life as a ransom for many (Matt 20:28)

The biblically literate will know that the Tabernacle of the Exodus looked forward in type to Jesus. God provided the tabernacle so that "My presence will go with you, and I will give you rest (Exod 33:14). Jesus is preparing a place for us "That where He is, there we may be also." A single gate was provided for entrance into the tabernacle entrance. Jesus said "I am the door." The sacrifice made and the brazen altar in which there is "no remission of sins except by the shedding of blood" would point to the atoning cross of Jesus. A laver was provided for the ceremonial washing of the priest who must be clean in order to come into the presence of God. *"If we confess our sins, He is faithful and righteous to forgive us our sins and to cleanse us from all unrighteousness"* (1 John 1:9). Sinless and cleansed the high priest was then allowed to enter into the sanctuary where there were positioned three important furnishings. The first was the menorah which pointed to "the light of the world," which is Jesus. Then there was the table of showbread which pointed to Jesus as "the Bread of Life, and lastly the golden altar of incense symbolizing the prayers and intercession of the people going up to God as a sweet fragrance. This pointed to Christ who is our intercessor before God the Father. From there, the inner room called "the Holy of Holies" was a representation of heaven itself, to be entered only by the pure in heart. This inner sanctuary was shielded from the eye of those outside by a curtain, a curtain which was ripped from top to bottom with the crucifixion of Jesus. Jesus, as our high priest, went before us on our behalf. Within was the Arc of the Covenant. Inside it God had commanded three items to be placed: a golden pot of manna, Aaron's staff that had budded, and the two stone tablets on which the Ten Commandments were written. The manna was an uncomfortable reminder that despite their grumbling in the wilderness, God had provided this "bread from heaven." Aaron's staff that had budded reminded them that the people out of jealousy had rebelled against Aaron as their high priest. On more than one occasion they had rejected God's authority. The Ten Commandments, of course, represented God's conditional covenant with Israel:

> "Now if you obey me fully and keep my covenant, then out of all nations you will be my treasured possession. Although the whole earth is mine, you will be for me a kingdom of priests and a holy nation" (Exod 19:5–6).

Of course, the people did not keep their end of the covenant and that brought judgement upon them. Yet, because of God's mercy, they were restored. God provided a New Covenant for them:

> Behold, the days are coming, says the LORD, when I will make a new covenant with the house of Israel and with the house of Judah— not according to the covenant that I made with their fathers in the day that I took them by the hand to lead them out of the land of Egypt, My covenant which they broke, though I was a husband to them, says the LORD. But this is the covenant that I will make with the house of Israel after those days, says the LORD: I will put My law in their minds, and write it on their hearts; and I will be their God, and they shall be My people. No more shall every man teach his neighbor, and every man his brother, saying, 'Know the LORD,' for they all shall know Me, from the least of

them to the greatest of them, says the LORD. *For I will forgive their
iniquity, and their sin I will remember no more* (Jer 31:31–34).

The writer of Hebrews after reminding us of what we have reviewed
above, explains that Christ has become our "high priest." If we were
Hebrew, we should see that He is the fulfillment of all that was in the
Old Testament "Christ concealed."

> *Christ is the mediator of a new covenant, that those who are
> called may receive the promised eternal inheritance—now
> that he has died as a ransom to set them free from the sins
> committed under the first covenant* (Heb 9:15).

The crucifixion is described in the Bible in various ways, or
(more precisely) is translated with several English descriptions. In
the above instance the Greek word *'lutron,'* appearing only in
Matthew and Mark, refers to the payment of a price in order to
purchase the freedom of a slave. Here Jesus is described as paying
with his own life, in substitution for our own penalty, to set us free
from the curse of death.

In other places in the New Testament the Greek word *'hilasmos'*
or *'hilasterion'* is used to refer to the mercy seat (or place of
satisfaction) where God's wrath toward sin is satisfied (Rom 3:25;
Heb 9:5). With the mercy seat of the tabernacle the covering of sin
was through the substitutionary blood of an innocent animal. It is
less correctly translated "propitiation" or "reconciliation" which
means "to appease God." Other translations give the better
rendering "expiation." Expiation carries the meaning "to repair the
wrong done."

In 1 John 2:2 and 4:10 the word *'hilasmos'* is often translated
"atonement". It is poor exegesis to embrace the English accident of
"At-One-Ment" where all meaning of Jesus' sacrifice is lost. I am

told that it does not translate easily, and at times is also translated "expiation" or "propitiation."

Since ransom, substitution, expiation, atonement and propitiation all have slightly different connotations and associations, the translation choice has created doctrinal differences. When I used the word "propitiation" with my Greek Orthodox scholar friend, he immediately corrected me, explaining that Christ's death was to set us free from the Law. This placed us under the new directive of Faith. We then must follow Him in obedience and respond by faith through good works. The cross does not save us, he told me, our good works by faith save us. Of course, I realized then that I would just avoid the argument and thanked him for his insight.

Where we agree is that there is a regeneration wrought by the Holy Spirit. John Wesley said this: "The new birth is that great change which God works in the soul when He brings it into life; when He raises from the death of sin to the life of righteousness It is the change wrought in the whole soul by the Almighty Spirit of God when it is created anew in Christ Jesus, when it is renewed after the image of God in righteousness and true holiness." Dr. Hanna said, "Regeneration is the mighty change in man, wrought by the Holy Spirit, by which the dominion which sin had over him in his natural state, and which he deplores and struggles against in his penitent state, is broken and demolished; so that with full choice of will and the energy of right assertion he serves God freely and runs in the way of His commandments." Someone has said that regeneration is defined as an ingeneration of divine life; a sudden process by which man passes from spiritual death to a spiritual life through the quickening power of God's Holy Spirit. In regeneration one passes from a state of death to a state of spiritual life; from a state of guilt to a state of "forgiveness;" from a state of pollution – that is, the pollution acquired by his own acts of disobedience against the laws of God – to a state of conscious cleansing; that is, a cleansing from acquired pollution. Regeneration, or conversion, used in a broad sense, may be defined, therefore, as the act of the Holy Spirit in answer to faith by which spiritual life is imparted to a dead soul, his sins are freely forgiven him, and the moral corruption accumulated through his sins taken away. The man stands as a new creature in Christ Jesus; old things have passed away and all things become new. He recognizes that he is no longer a friend to the world but God's child, separated from all that is evil and committed to obedience to God's holy commandments.[19]

My position is that the cross was the effective expression of God's saving grace. When we accept by faith this blood sacrifice of the only sinless man that ever lived, the perfect atonement for our sin, when we believe in Him who gave His life a ransom for many, we are saved. We are born again. We are set free from the law of sin and death. We will then respond in love and obedience with deep gratitude by a life of devotion and service to Him. We will take up our cross daily and follow Him. We have no power in ourselves to save ourselves, yet we pay the price of giving up everything, even our lives, for the sake of this divine man, Christ Jesus, who emptied Himself, walked among us and laid down His life's blood for us. This was a finished work of grace. "It is finished," He said, and then He committed His spirit into God's hands.

This grace was not cheap. And we must not cheapen it by taking it for granted or being careless about our own sin. We must respond by allowing Him to mold us into His own image. And we must not cheapen His expiation by pretending to earn our salvation through good works. In order to receive His great gift of love we must respond in faith and obedience leading to good works. Without the faith response there is little evidence that we are saved.

I Lay My Sins on Jesus

Horatius Bonar, 1843

I lay my sins on Jesus, the spotless Lamb of God;
He bears them all, and frees us from the accursed load.
I bring my guilt to Jesus to wash my crimson stains
White in His blood most precious, till not a spot remains.

To God Be the Glory

Crosby and Doane, 1875

To God be the glory – great things He hath done:
So loved he the world that he gave us His Son,
Who yielded his life an atonement for sin,
And opened the life-gate that all may go in.
O perfect redemption, the purchase of blood –
To every believer, the promise of God!
The vilest offender who truly believes,
That moment from Jesus a pardon receives.

CHAPTER 16

WORKS (the Faith Response)

For as the body without the spirit is dead, so faith without works is dead also (James 2:26).

For the grace of God that brings salvation has appeared to all men, teaching us that, denying ungodliness and worldly lusts, we should live soberly, righteously, and godly in the present age, looking for the blessed hope and glorious appearing of our great God and Savior Jesus Christ, who gave Himself for us, that He might redeem us from every lawless deed and purify for Himself His own special people, zealous for good works (Titus 2:11–14).

While the issue of whether or not you can earn your salvation by good works is settled for many, the issue of whether good works should follow those who have believed is another consideration. The primary motivation for good works is thanksgiving. Having been given so much I could not earn, it is unimaginable that I would sit on my laurels and give nothing back to Jesus. Jesus taught to give to others on His behalf: *"And the King will answer and say to them, 'Assuredly, I say to you, inasmuch as you did it to one of the least of these My brethren, you did it to Me.'"* (Matt 25:40). It is gratifying to know that He has given something for us to give away. It is more than time, talent and treasure that we have to give, it is ourselves.

You shall receive power when the Holy Spirit has come upon you; and you shall be witnesses to Me in

That there is power in the Christian life for ministry that is given to overcome, to fill others' needs, to testify to God's goodness, to feed the hungry, give to the poor and clothe the naked, is a fact missed by many believers. If we have no financial resources to give in that manner, we have other ways to serve, no time or talent, then we can give of ourselves. The other great stimulator for service to others is love, divine love received, love for others given. This was a wonderful fruit given me by the Holy Spirit. That I love others is for me confirmation of his transforming grace. I did not have this love before. It simply came from Him. Along with it I lost my fear of people. To pursue people for Jesus' sake is now what gives me purpose. No debate, it now comes naturally. I want to go and do for Him.

And Jesus came and spoke to them, saying, "All authority has been given to Me in heaven and on earth. Go therefore and make disciples of all the nations, baptizing them in the name of the Father and of the Son and of the Holy Spirit, teaching them to observe all things that I have commanded you; and lo, I am with you always, even to the end of the age" (Matt 28:18–20).

Your work may be to pray. Jesus delegates His authority:

And whatever you ask in My name, that I will do, that the Father may be glorified in the Son. If you ask anything in My name, I will do it (John 14:13–14).

He said to pray for workers to go out into the field which is white onto harvest. Both the prayer for the workers and the work which they will do are needed. Jesus said, "I must work the works of Him who sent Me while it is day; *the* night is coming when no one can work. Your work may be manual labor or it may be music in worship or it may be cooking for others. My favorite of the gifts of the Spirit is the gift of "helps" (1 Cor 12:28). How often have I been the "chairman" (which is to say setting up chairs) or cleaning up after an event. Our work may be ministry, as in speaking or writing or singing. It may be hospital, shut-in or prison visitation. We all have something we can do in Jesus name by which we can bring glory to Jesus.

It is important for us to heed Jesus' admonition to not pray, fast and give in order to be seen by men. This is an important part of the Sermon on the Mount of Matthew 5-7.

> *Take heed that you do not do your charitable deeds before men, to be seen by them. Otherwise you have no reward from your Father in heaven. Therefore, when you do a charitable deed, do not sound a trumpet before you as the hypocrites do in the synagogues and in the streets, that they may have glory from men. Assuredly, I say to you, they have their reward. But when you do a charitable deed, do not let your left hand know what your right hand is doing, that your charitable deed may be in secret; and your Father who sees in secret will Himself reward you openly (Matt 6:1-4).*

The issue is that motivation to bring glory to ourselves rather than to Christ. Some have called this "vainglory." Jesus tells us that deeds done with the intention of impressing men are worthless in His sight (Matt 6:2). These works are the "wood, hay and straw" mentioned in 1 Corinthians 3:12. What kinds of rewards will we receive when we are judged? It is interesting that God Himself promises to give rewards for our work. I believe there will be a reward ceremony of sorts in heaven with the judgement seat of Christ. There will be bema (crowns) which will be awarded. Consider these passages in Scripture:

1. Incorruptible Crown (The Victor's Crown)

    And everyone who competes for the prize is temperate in all things. Now they do it to obtain a perishable crown, but we for an imperishable crown (1 Cor 9:25).

2. Crown of Life (The Martyr's Crown)

    Do not fear any of those things which you are about to suffer. Indeed, the devil is about to throw some of you into prison, that you may be tested, and you will have tribulation ten days. Be faithful until death, and I will give you the crown of life (Rev 2:10).

3. Crown of Glory (Elder's Crown)

    Shepherd the flock of God which is among you, serving as overseers, not by compulsion but willingly, not for dishonest gain but eagerly; nor as being lords over those entrusted to you, but being examples to the flock; and when the Chief Shepherd appears, you will receive the crown of glory that does not fade away (1 Pet 5:2–4).

4. Crown of Righteousness (For those who love His appearing)

    Finally, there is laid up for me the crown of righteousness, which the Lord, the righteous Judge, will give to me on that Day, and not to me only but also to all who have loved his appearing (2 Tim 4:8).

5. Crown of Rejoicing (Soul Winner's Crown)

For what is our hope, or joy, or crown of rejoicing? Is it not even you in the presence of our Lord Jesus Christ at His coming? For you are our glory and joy (1 Thes 2:19-20).

Of course it is the 24 elders who will cast their crowns at the feet of Jesus. However, if I get a chance, and I have a crown, I will do the same, for He is worthy to receive glory, honor and power.

YOUR LOVE COMPELS ME
Doug Holck, 1982

Your love compels me Lord,
To give as You would give,
To speak as You would speak,
To live as You would live.
Your love compels me Lord,
To see as You would see,
To serve as You would serve,
To be what You would be.

I'LL GO WHERE YOU WANT ME TO GO
Brown, Prior & Rounsefell, 1894

There's surely somewhere a lowly place
In earth's harvest fields so wide
Where I may labor thro' life's short day

For Jesus the Crucified.
So trusting my all to Thy tender care,
And knowing Thou lovest me,
I'll do Thy will with a heart sincere.
I'll be what You want me to be.

CHAPTER 17
SANCTIFICATION (Glorious Freedom) [20]

When the Holy "Guest" abides within
– Samuel Logan Brengle

In my Preface I mentioned a valuable book I possess published by Samuel Logan Brengle in 1934. In his third chapter he speaks of "The Guest of the Soul." I quote him liberally here:

A friend of mine said recently, "I like the term, 'Holy ghost,' for the word Ghost in the old Saxon was the same as the word for Guest." Whether that be so or not, it may certainly be said that the Holy Ghost is the Holy Guest. He has come into the world and visits every heart, seeking admittance as a guest. He may come to the soul unbidden, but He will not come in unbidden. He may be unwelcome. He may be refused admission and turned away. But He comes. He is in the world like Noah' dove, looking for an abiding-place. He comes as a Guest, but as an abiding one, if received. He forces Himself on no one. He waits for the open door and the invitation.

He comes gently. He comes in love. He comes on a mission of infinite good will, of mercy and peace and helpfulness and joy. He is the Advocate of the Father and of the Son to us men. He represents and executes the redemptive plans and purpose of the Triune God. As my old teacher, Daniel Steele (1824-1914), wrote, "He is the Executive of the Godhead."...

When the Holy Ghost becomes the holy Guest in the yielded welcoming heart, He dwells there ungrieved and with delight. "As the bridegroom rejoiceth over the bride (Isa 62:5). He rejoices over that soul, while the soul has sweet, ennobling, purifying fellowship and communion with its Lord. He illuminates that soul; purifies, sanctifies, empowers it; instructs it, comforts it, protects it, adjust it to all circumstances and crosses, and fits it for effective service, patient suffering, and willing sacrifice....

When the Holy Guest abides within, the soul does not shun the way of the Cross, nor seek great things for itself. It is content to serve in lowly as in lofty ways, in obscure and hidden places as in open and conspicuous places where waits applause. To wash a poor disciple's feet is as great a joy as to command an army, to follow as to lead, to serve as to rule – when the Holy Guest abides within the soul. Then the soul does not contend for or grasp and hold fast to place and power....

Finally, the great work of this holy Guest is to exalt Jesus; to glorify Him who humbled himself unto the shameful and agonizing death of the cross; to make us to see Him in all His beauty; to knit our hearts to Him in faith and love and loyalty, conform us to His image and fit us for His work.[21]

I prefer Brengle's reference to the "Holy Guest" above the word 'sanctification,' however defer to the more broadly used term. Right up front let me deal with the terminology regarding the word *'Sanctification.'* Sanctification means to be separated unto holiness. It should not be understood as the mere absence of sin. Rather, it should be defined by the presence of things we must/can do as holy people. The word is used for all of the following experiences:

Initial Sanctification – Regeneration is the response to prevenient grace, to be saved, born again. God begins the process of calling unto holiness. This is imparted righteousness (vs. imputed that some believe, i.e. the holiness of God).

Entire Sanctification – There is a crisis experience where He sanctifies us through and through; He makes us righteous from inside out as we consecrate our lives wholly to Him. This is a call to decision, a second point of decision in one's life where God draws us into a deeper decision.

Progressive Sanctification – Then continuing everyday of our lives growing us into His image (we are being sanctified). this is on-going sanctification.

Final Sanctification – This is when we are resurrected to be with Him, for we shall see Him as He is and be like Him in our glorification.

There is a sin problem within Christians after conversion. God has called the Christian to radical holiness, radical love, radical obedience, radical humility, radical forgiveness, radical unselfishness, and radical servanthood. Jesus said, "You are to be perfect, as your heavenly Father is perfect" (Matt 5:48). Jesus spoke often about being totally sold out to God. He said that becoming a Christian is like selling all you have and taking the money to buy a valuable pearl. Or it's like taking all your money to buy a piece of property that has buried treasure on it. Or, consider the "take up his cross" passage (Matt 10:38). Why would He ask us to become so sold out, so completely committed to Christ if we were incapable of such devotion? The problem is that we Christians forget that we have made our commitments, falter in our promises and give in to temptation. We hurt ourselves and others at times (when we should be loving them). These things must bring much grief to the Savior who died for us! "Wretched man that I am! Who will set me free from the body of this death?" writes the Apostle Paul. "But thanks be to God who gives us the victory through our Lord Jesus Christ" (1 Cor 15:57). Let's read what the Apostle John writes to Christians:

> *"I am writing these things to you that you may not sin.*
> *And if anyone does sin, we have an Advocate with the*
> *Father, Jesus Christ the righteous (1 John 2:1).*

It is good to know that the One who has placed such a great challenge before us is also our Advocate. It seems almost too easy to sin with impunity. Paul asks the inevitable question:

James speaks of the Christian who is "double minded, unstable in all his ways" (James 1:6-8; 4:8). This indicates a heart that needs to be purified. There is a danger in being one who is weak in the faith. Such are more vulnerable to Satan's attacks; they are influenced by "every wind of doctrine." They cause problems for other Christians rather than encouraging them and they are of little use in winning others to Christ. "From the same mouth come both blessing and cursing. Brethren, these things ought not to be," said James (James 3:10). Some have coined the phrase "carnal Christian" for this kind of Christian. Whether a Christian sins or not, it seems to be our common experience that after we are saved, we become deeply aware of our need for something more, of a remaining hindrance to further spiritual growth, of an inner struggle with ourselves. Paul Explains in Romans, chapters 5-7, that the Spirit is in conflict with our sinful nature, so that we do not do what we want to do.

What is the sin principle with which we were born? It is Adamic depravity. We were born with a propensity to sin. This sin nature is what caused us to sin in the first place. It was our nature to doubt God. It was our nature to disobey God. It was our nature to rebel against God. And, it was our nature to pervert God's purposes. The good news is that God has provided the remedy through Entire Sanctification, the second work of grace. What is our basis for this belief?

You might ask, "Why Do We Believe in the Second Work of Grace?" First, there is a psychological basis for entire sanctification. When we came to the Lord to be saved, our frame of mind was that of a repentant rebel who approached God, begging for forgiveness. We had been a disobedient sinner, not a child of God. We confessed our belief in the efficacious blood of Jesus Christ and trusted Him to cleanse us from our committed sins. God remembered them against us no more and wrote our names in the Lamb's Book of Life. As a result a heavy load of guilt and shame was removed from our shoulders and we were set free from sin's bondage and death. A place in heaven is prepared for us. But there comes a time when God places a hunger in our heart for something more.

As believers, Christians already forgiven of our sins, when we come asking God for entire sanctification, our psychological frame of mind is quite different. We do not repent of our sins and turn from them, since that has already been done. We yield ourselves to God as His children, willing to be altogether donated to God's cause. We are open to God for His use. Already born again, we want the sin nature to be cleansed away by Christ's baptism with the Holy Spirit so that we can serve God in an established relationship and be used of Him more powerfully in service to other persons. Our frame of mind is vastly different from that of an unbeliever seeking forgiveness; and surely it would be at least next to impossible to have at the same time the two states of mind that are appropriate for receiving the two works of grace.

Secondly, there is a theological basis for entire sanctification. There are two types of sin from which the two works of grace deliver us: 1) <u>acts of sin</u> and 2) <u>Adamic depravity</u>. Acts of sin require forgiveness. But we are not culpable for Adamic depravity. It does not require forgiveness, because we were born with it. We would never enter into eternal perdition due to it alone. But as a state it needs to be cleansed away, to be expelled, destroyed, done away with. This occurs in the second work of grace, when believers are granted freedom from sin (Rom 6:18; 8:1-2); when the body of sin, the state of sin, is destroyed; when the Adamic depravity, which Paul often refers to as the *sarx*, is "crucified" (Gal 5:24); when believers are "circumcised, in the putting off of the sinful nature, not with a circumcision done by the hands of men but with the circumcision done by Christ" (Col 2:11).

Furthermore, there is a strong Scriptural basis for entire sanctification. Consider first of all the two-work passages (both works mentioned in the same scripture).

> *I indeed baptize you with water unto repentance, but He who is coming after me is mightier than I, whose sandals I am not worthy to carry. He will baptize you with the Holy Spirit and fire (Matt 3:11; also in Mark 1:7-8; Luke 3:16-17, and John 1:26-27)*

> *Therefore, having been justified by faith, we have peace with God through our Lord Jesus Christ, through whom also we have access by faith into this grace in which we stand, and rejoice in hope of the glory of God. And not only that, but we also glory in tribulations, knowing that tribulation produces perseverance; and*

perseverance, character; and character, hope. Now hope does not disappoint, because the love of God has been poured out in our hearts by the Holy Spirit who was given to us (Rom 5:1–5)

knowing this, that our old man was crucified with Him, that the body of sin might be done away with, that we should no longer be slaves of sin (Rom 6:6)

In Him you also trusted, after you heard the word of truth, the gospel of your salvation; in whom also, having believed, you were sealed with the Holy Spirit of promise (Eph 1:13)

Husbands, love your wives, just as Christ also loved the church and gave Himself for her, that He might sanctify and cleanse her with the washing of water by the word, that He might present her to Himself a glorious church, not having spot or wrinkle or any such thing, but that she should be holy and without blemish (Eph 5:25–27)

Draw near to God and He will draw near to you. Cleanse your hands, you sinners; and purify your hearts, you double-minded (James 4:8).

Other passages of larger compass also teach two works of grace. Under the preaching of Philip at Samaria, people "believed" and were baptized in water (Acts 8:12-17). Still later, when Peter and John arrived, they "prayed for them that they might receive the Holy Spirit. Then they placed their hands on them, and they received the Holy Spirit."

In 1 Thessalonians we find Paul addressing Christians whom he has highly commended, teaching them that something is lacking in their faith (3:10). In (3:13) Paul writes, "May he 'establish,'[NASB] your hearts so that you will be blameless and holy in the presence of our God and Father." He soon adds in (4:3), "It is God's will that you should be sanctified." And before long he is saying, "May God himself, the God of Peace, sanctify you through and through"(5:23).

Entire sanctification happens in a moment of time. Analogous to regeneration, entire sanctification is by faith and occurs instantaneously. If it were by "growth in grace" it would be by works or gradual maturity. While there is growth in grace, it is not the same as sanctification which accelerates this growth. The biblical symbols of sanctification do not suggest a long process.

- Baptized with the Holy Spirit (Acts 1:5)
- Filled with the Holy Spirit (Acts 2:4)
- Holy Spirit Fell on them (Acts 10:44)
- Crucifixion of our old self (Rom 6:6; Gal 5:24)
- Circumcision of the heart (Rom 2:29; Col 2:11)
- Anointed by God (2 Cor 1:21)
- Sealed with the Holy Spirit (2 Cor 1:22; Eph 1:13; 4:30)

Furthermore, the New Testament grammar indicates the immediacy of entire sanctification. The Greek aorist tense suggests an event occurring at a moment in time (i.e. without duration):

- *'supply, complete, perfect'* (1 Thes 3:10)
- *'establish'* in holiness (1 Thes 3:13)
- *'sanctify'* them in the truth (John 17:17)
- *'sanctify'* you entirely (1 Thes 5:23)
- *'giving'* them the Holy Spirit (Acts 15:8-9)
- *'bears witness'* to us (Heb 10:14-15)

Entire Sanctification Brings About a Dramatic Life Change. R.T. Williams offers this description: *"A sanctified man – just a man, not an angel, but a man – a man with all of his appetites and passions that are legitimate and normal. These powers are necessarily God-given and natural to the human race. These are not only divinely bestowed, but are to be kept as an essential part of human nature and human life. God gave them for a purpose, and if they had never been degraded by sin and prostituted to unnatural and abnormal uses, they would have been held as sacred and useful. A sanctified man therefore is a man, just a man; not an angel, but a man with all of his appetites and passions that are normal and legitimate; a man that is consecrated to God body, soul and spirit; a man whose heart has been cleansed from all sin and filled with the love of God so that he is enabled by the circumcision of the heart to love God with all of his soul powers, and his neighbor as himself. He is a man who possesses the appetites, the passions, the physical and mental powers with which God originally made him; who has consecrated all to God and His service; whose consecration has been accepted, his heart purified, and filled with divine love and possessed by divine personality. He now stands a consecrated man, cleansed from all sin and filled with God and is able to fulfill the law of love in his attitude both toward God and man."* [22]

Sanctification carries two meanings, that of cleansing and that of setting aside for special use. Both apply in this experience. The most basic component of entire sanctification is the cleansing of the sin principle. With the cleansing of natural depravity, the struggle is outward and united with the heart and mind of God as the light exposes every dark corner where sin used to hide. Entire sanctification breaks the power of sin. Our cleansing enables us to live victoriously in this life and to be used of God in new ways.

> *For if we live, we live to the Lord; and if we die, we die*
> *to the Lord. Therefore, whether we live or die, we are*
> *the Lord's* (Rom 14:8).

I have been crucified with Christ; it is no longer I who live, but Christ lives in me; and the life which I now live in the flesh I live by faith in the Son of God, who loved me and gave Himself for me (Gal 2:20).

The baptism with the Holy Spirit effects entire sanctification. In this baptism the Holy Spirit is poured out upon the believer. The Spirit then indwells the believer pervasively. Reiterating Matt 3:11,

I indeed baptize you with water unto repentance, but He who is coming after me is mightier than I, whose sandals I am not worthy to carry. He will baptize you with the Holy Spirit and fire (Matt 3:11).

And being assembled together with them, He commanded them not to depart from Jerusalem, but to wait for the Promise of the Father, "which," He said, "you have heard from Me; for John truly baptized with water, but you shall be baptized with the Holy Spirit not many days from now." ... And they were all filled with the Holy Spirit and began to speak with other tongues, as the Spirit gave them utterance (Acts 1:4–5; 2:4).

Not only purity, but power is associated with the baptism with the Holy Spirit, especially power for witnessing:

But you shall receive power when the Holy Spirit has come upon you; and you shall be witnesses to Me in Jerusalem, and in all Judea and Samaria, and to the end of the earth (Acts 1:8).

Entire sanctification is described in scripture as a sealing:

Now He who establishes us with you in Christ and has anointed us is God, who also has sealed us and given us the Spirit in our hearts as a guarantee (2 Cor 1:21–22).

In Him you also trusted, after you heard the word of truth, the gospel of your salvation; in whom also, having believed, you were sealed with the Holy Spirit of promise, who is the guarantee of our inheritance until the redemption of the purchased possession, to the praise of His glory.... And do not grieve the Holy Spirit of God, by whom you were sealed for the day of redemption (Eph 1:13–14; 4:30).

The seal is the promised Holy Spirit, given as a pledge, an earnest, a deposit guaranteeing our inheritance. Sealing suggests ownership, and it is our privilege to belong to Him.

He who overcomes, I will make him a pillar in the temple of My God, and he shall go out no more. I will write on him the name of My God and the name of the city of My God, the New Jerusalem, which comes down out of heaven from My God. And I will write on him My new name (Rev 3:12).

It is only when the recalcitrant original sin is cleansed that the fullness of God's love can fill the heart and Christian growth toward a rich and fruitful maturity can best take place. W.T. Purkiser puts it this way: "The sanctifying grace of God is sufficient to free the Christian heart from the power and presence of inner sin, to fill it with pure love for God and man, and to impart power for Christian life in the present world."

> *Therefore, leaving the discussion of the elementary principles of Christ, let us go on to perfection, not laying again the foundation of repentance from dead works and of faith toward God, of the doctrine of baptisms, of laying on of hands, of resurrection of the dead, and of eternal judgment. And this we will do if God permits.... For the earth which drinks in the rain that often comes upon it, and bears herbs useful for those by whom it is cultivated, receives blessing from God; ...But, beloved, we are confident of better things concerning you, yes, things that accompany salvation, though we speak in this manner* (Heb 6:1-3, 7, 9).

Perhaps most misunderstood about this work of grace is the word "perfection." Having "gone on to perfection" (Heb 6:1) and answered the call of Christ to "be ye perfect even as your Heavenly Father is perfect" (Matt 5:48), we are made perfect only in the sense that carnality has been rendered foreign to our sanctified heart. But we are not perfect in our judgment or in ethical conduct. In scripture the word 'perfection' seems to be used as a synonym for the Greek '*pneumatikoi*,' the "spiritual ones," in distinction from carnal Christians (1 Cor 3:1*ff*). Paul was to have had special meetings with the '*hoi teleioi*,' the "perfect ones," according to scripture   (1 Cor 2:6, 12; 14:16, 23). These are Christians who have received cleansing from Adamic sin through Christ's Spirit baptism. Perfect conduct is certainly not possible in this life. (Heb 6:1; Matt 5:48; 1 Cor 2:6,12; 1 Cor 14:16,23)

Entire sanctification is referred to as "the establishing grace" (1 Thes 3:13; Rom 5:1-2).   The Christian who has been sanctified wholly can fall completely from grace, but just as surely, he is enabled not to fall from grace. In fellowship with the empowering, teaching, filling Holy Spirit, backsliding is not very likely. Why? Because Christ paid such a great price for your salvation, He will not so easily leave you. This is conditional upon whether a man has yielded to the direction of the Holy Spirit. So, it is not so much to say we have all of Him as it is to know that He has all of us.

The second work of grace enables us to love God and others with all our heart and mind and soul and strength (Deut 30:6; Matt 26:39). Wesley often called the second blessing "perfect love" (1 John 4:8).

Historically, from Wesley through Bresee, holiness people have answered the call to feed and clothe the poor, minister to the sick and care for those who are outcast from society (Isaiah 58). Additionally, holiness people have always maintained large world mission ministries. The utter consecration to God's use, in order to receive and maintain entire sanctification, figures in both the willingness for missionary service and sacrificial giving for its support (Matt 28:19; Acts 1:8).

When God searches for a man or woman to work in His vineyard, He does not ask, "Has he great natural abilities? Is she thoroughly educated? Is he a fine singer? Is she eloquent in prayer?" Rather He asks, "Is his heart perfect toward Me? Is she holy? Does he love much? Is she willing to walk by faith and not be sight? Does he love Me so much and has he such childlike confidence in My love for him that he can trust Me to use him when he doesn't see any sign that I am using him? Will she be weary and faint when I correct her and try to fit her for greater usefulness? Or will she, like Job, cry out, 'Though He slay me, yet will I turst in Him' (Job 13:15)? Does he search My Word, and 'meditate on it day and night' in order to 'be sure to obey everything written in it' (Josh 1:8)? Does he wait on Me for My counsel and seek in everything to be led by My Spirit? Or is he stubborn and self-willed, like the horse and the mule, which have to be held in with bit and bridle, so that I cannot 'guide him with mine eye' (Psa 32:8)? Is she a people-pleaser and a time-server, or is she willing to wait for her reward, seeking solely for 'the honor that comes from the only God' (John 5:44)? Does he 'preach the word' and is he 'ready in season and out of season' (2 Tim 4:2)? Is she meek and lowly in heart and humble?" [23]

This desire to "be separate" from that which is worldly in order to practice Christian discipline and a life of service caused early Wesleyans to be dubbed "Methodists." In the American Holiness Movement alcohol and tobacco have often been banned, as has much in the theater, in films, in music, and in dance. People were to live modestly and to be holy "in life and in look." (Rom 12:1-2; 1 Cor 6:12-20; 1 Thes 5:21-22; 1 John 2:15-17) Yet, it has concerned many that these things lead to an atmosphere of legalism. If that be true it may steal the freedom in the Holy Spirit. You cannot be sanctified by avoiding sin.

Acts 15:8-9 suggests, as do other passages, that there is a witness of the Holy Spirit to the work of entire sanctification. Rev. Beverly Carradine tells of a thrilling and ecstatic experience as the Holy Spirit bore witness to his sanctification.[24] We find however, that not everyone has such an ecstatic experience and that we ought not be looking for such manifestation so much as the wonderful assurance the Holy Spirit gives. Wesley taught that besides the direct witness of the Spirit to our hearts, there is an indirect witness from the "fruits" of our life. But the direct witness is primary. We should not rest on any supposed fruit of the spirit, and even more importantly on some manifestation of the spirit as in the exercise of the gifts of the Spirit, but seek entire sanctification, and keep on seeking, until the Holy Spirit has witnessed of the grace in our hearts.

> *But the Holy Spirit also witnesses to us; for after He had said before, "This is the covenant that I will make with them after those days," says the LORD: "I will put My laws into their hearts, and in their minds I will write them"* (Heb 10:15-16).

Furthermore, there is an indirect witness of walking by the Spirit (Gal 5:16-17, 25). He is sanctified holy who can never love God enough and whose adoration for Him is unceasing; who loves people with a great love and cares little for things; who prays earnestly for people and follows up in practical ways to help them; who reveres the indwelling Holy Spirit and waits upon the Lord; who battles constantly against indwelling sin and cares for holiness; who only grows spiritually stronger and sweeter through life's adversities; who pleads God's promises waiting expectantly for their fulfillment; who practices self-discipline maturely and thoughtfully; who cares little for praise and vain glory, but redirects it toward God; whose humility lubricates every facet of his accomplishment; who waits expectantly for Jesus' commendation, "*Well done, thou good and faithful servant.*"

How can a person be sanctified? Firstly, the believer should understand what is offered. He should ask God to reveal the need for removal of the propensity to sin. He must feel the need to be sanctified entirely in order to have faith for baptism with the Holy Spirit. If one is doubtful, He must ask God for understanding. Then one should expect to receive this blessing in accordance with God's promise. He should read the scripture involved. However, one should not read and study the Word to get a mass of knowledge in the head but a flame of love in the heart. "Knowledge puffs up while love builds up" (1 Cor 8:1). Read it to fuel affection and to find food for reflection, direction for judgment, and guidance for conscience. Read it not that you may know but that you may do.[25] He should also read holiness literature regarding the fully committed life. He should empty himself of all other ambitions. He should be willing to deny himself and to live sacrificially. He should break any personal ties that would hinder the sovereignty of Christ, e.g. another person's unhealthy sovereignty over him. He should be ready to strengthen other relationships that God may desire for him. Then, he must consecrate himself completely. This is yielding oneself to God to be used where, how, and with whom He wills. In consecration we make a whole response to God, donating ourselves as His children to His service. (Rom 12:1). Finally, he must receive it by faith. This is the final most crucial step in receiving entire sanctification. Actually, this is the one step that is always necessary. What will follow will propel us to love and care for others.

So God, who knows the heart, acknowledged them by giving them the Holy Spirit, just as He did to us, and made no distinction between us and them, purifying their hearts by faith... "Then I asked, 'Who are you, Lord?'... 'I am Jesus, whom you are persecuting,' the Lord replied. 'Now get up and stand on your feet. I have appeared to you to appoint you as a servant and as a witness... to open their eyes, in order to turn them from darkness to light, and from the power of Satan to God, that they may receive forgiveness of sins and an inheritance among those who are sanctified by faith in Me. (Acts 15:8-9; 26:15-18).*

I Want to Be Like Jesus

Chisholm & Ives, 1945

I have one deep, supreme desire –
That I may be like Jesus.
To this I fervently aspire –
That I may be like Jesus.
I want my heart His throne to be,
So that a watching world may see
His likeness shining forth in me.
I want to be like Jesus.
He spent His life in doing good;
I want to be like Jesus.

In lowly paths of service trod;
I want to be like Jesus.
He sympathized with hearts distressed,
He spoke the words that cheered and blessed,
He welcomed sinners to His breast.
I want to be like Jesus.
A holy, harmless life He led;
I want to be like Jesus.
The Father's will – his drink and bread;
I want to be like Jesus.
And when at last he comes to die,
"Forgive them, Father," hear Him cry
For those who taunt and crucify.
I want to be like Jesus.
O perfect life of Christ, my Lord!
I want to be like Jesus.
My recompense and my reward,
That I may be like Jesus.
His Spirit fill my hung'ring soul,
His power all my life control.
My deepest prayer, my highest goal –
That I may be like Jesus.

Have Thine Own Way, Lord
Pollard, 1902 & Stebbins, 1907

Have Thine own way, Lord! Have Thine own way!
Thou art the potter; I am the clay.
Mold me and make me after Thy will,
While I am waiting, yielded and still.
Have Thine own way, Lord! Have Thine own way!
Search me and try me, Master, today.

Whiter than snow, Lord, wash me just now,
As in Thy presence humbly I bow.
Have Thine own way, Lord! Have Thine own way!
Hold o'er my being absolute sway!
Fill with Thy Spirit till all shall see
Christ only, always living in me

O For a Heart to Praise My God
Charles Wesley - 1742

O for a heart to praise my God,
A heart from sin set free,
A heart that always feels Thy blood
So freely shed for me.
A heart resigned, submissive, meek,
My great Redeemer's throne,
Where only Christ is heard to speak,
Where Jesus reigns alone.
O for a lowly contrite heart,
Believing, true, and clean,
Which neither life nor death can part
From Him that dwells within.
A heart in ev'ry thought renewed
And full of love divine,
Perfect and right and pure and good–
A copy, Lord, of Thine.
Thy nature, gracious Lord, impart;
Come quickly from above;
Write Thy new name upon my heart,
Thy new, best name of Love.

NOTES

Chapter 2 – Holiness (The Divine Challenge)

1. Samuel Logan Brengle, *The Heart of Holiness*, Bob Hostetler, Gen. Ed. (Indianapolis, IN: Wesleyan Publishing House, 2016), 174.

2. Kenneth E. Jones, *Commitment to Holiness* (Prestonburg, KY: Reformation Publishers, 1985), 9-11.

3. Nina G. Gunter, *Christian Perfection : Transformation to Wholeness* (Kansas City, MO: The Foundry, 2000), 10-13.

4. Mildred Bangs Wynkoop, A Theology of Love (Kansas City, MO: Beacon Hill Press, 1972), 149-164.

5. Wynkoop, 23.

Chapter 3 – Free Moral Agency (Choice)

6. Norman Geisler, *"Freedom, Free Will and Determinism"* in *Evangelical Dictionary of Theology*, 2nd Ed. (Grand Rapids, MI: Baker Academic, 2001), 470.

7. J. Kenneth Grider, *A Wesleyan Holiness Theology* (Kansas City, MO: Beacon Hill Press, 1994), 244.

Chapter 5 – Exactly What Did I Do? (A Listing of Specific Sins)

8. Samuel L. Brengle, *The Guest of the Soul*, (London: Marshall, Morgan & Scott, 1934), 18-20.

Chapter 6 – God's Wrath & Withdrawal (The Terrifying Warning)

9. Much of the content of this chapter taken from: Paul M. Ethington, *God's Terrifying Warning: His Mercy & His Judgment* (Kendall Direct Publishing, 2019).

10. Walter C. Kaiser Jr., *The Promise Plan of God* (Grand Rapids, MI: Zondervan, 2008), 108-109.

11. Kaiser, 108-109

12. Kaiser, 110.

13. Kaiser, 279.

Chapter 7 – The Blame Game (Original Sin)

14. R.T. Williams, *Sanctification: The Experience and the Ethics*, (Kansas City, MO: Nazarene Publishing House, 1928), 14.

Chapter 13 – Conviction of Sin (God's Standard)

15. James Nichols & W.R. Bagnall, ed. & trans., *James Arminius*, (Grand Rapids: Baker Book House, 1956), 1:526-27.

16. J.I. Packer, *Concise Theology* (Wheaton, IL: Tyndale House Publishers, 1993), 86.

Chapter 14 – Grace (Mercy Applied)

17. Charles Swindoll, *Grace Awakening*, (Dallas, TX: Word Publishing, 1990), 154.

Chapter 15 – Redemption (A Price to Be Paid)

18. Paul M. Ethington, *Stumbling Block or Corner Stone?* (Kendle Direct Publishing, 2020), Chapter 4 entire.

19. R.T. Williams, *Sanctification: The Experience and the Ethics*, (Kansas City, MO: Nazarene Publishing House, 1928), 13-14.

Chapter 17 – Sanctification (Glorious Freedom!)

20. Paul M. Ethington, *Stumbling Block*, Chapter 6 entire.

21. Brengle, *The Guest*, 58-65.

22. R.T. Williams, 76-77.

23. Brengle, *Helps to Holiness*, Bob Hostetler, Gen. Ed. (Indianapolis, IN: Wesleyan Publishing House, 2016), 70-71.

24. Beverly Carradine, Sanctification (Syracuse, NY: A.W. Hall, Publishers, 2905), 21.

25. Brengle, *The Heart*, 149.

BIBLIOGRAPHY

Brengle, Samuel L. *Helps to Holiness*, Bob Hostetler, Gen. Ed. Indianapolis, IN: Wesleyan Publishing House, 2016.

Brengle, Samuel L. *The Guest of the Soul.* London: Marshall, Morgan & Scott, 1934.

Brengle, Samuel L. *The Heart of Holiness*, Bob Hostetler, Gen. Ed. Indianapolis, IN: Wesleyan Publishing House, 2016.

Carradine, Beverly. *Sanctification.* Syracuse, NY: A.W. Hall, Publisher, 1905.

Ethington, Paul M. *God's Terrifying Warning: His Mercy & His Judgment.* Kendle Direct Publishing, 2019.

Ethington, Paul M. *Stumbling Block or Corner Stone?* Kendle Direct Publishing, 2020.

Geisler, Norman. "Freedom, Free Will and Determinism" in *Evangelical Dictionary of Theology*, 2nd Ed. Grand Rapids, MI: Baker Academic, 2001.

Grider, J. Kenneth. *A Wesleyan Holiness Theology.* Kansas City, MO: Beacon Hill Press, 1994.

Gunter, Nina G. *Christian Perfection: Transformation to Wholeness.* Kansas City, MO: The Foundry, 2000.

Jones, Kenneth E. *The Commitment to Holiness*. Prestonburg, KY: Reformation Publishers, 1985.

Kaiser, Walter C. Jr. *The Promise-Plan of God*. Grand Rapids, MI: Zondervan, 2008.

Leclerc, Diane. *Discovering Christian Holiness*. Kansas City, MO: Beacon Hill Press, 2010.

Nichols & W.R. Bagnall, ed. & trans. *James Arminius*. Grand Rapids, MI: Baker Book House, 1956.

Williams, R.T. *Sanctification: The Experience and the Ethics*. Kansas City, MO: Nazarene Publishing House, 1928.

Wyncoop, Mildred Bangs. *A Theology of Love: The Dynamic of Wesleyanism*. Kansas City, MO: Beacon Hill Press, 1972.

APPENDIX A
INDEX OF SCRIPTURES USED

Psalms

7:11	74
10:2–11	44
24:1–2	73
32:8	129
34:13	44
51:4	37
52:7	44
59:12	44
81:9	41
91:1–6	74
100:3	73
101:5	45
103:9	83
127:3–5	40

Proverbs

6:16–19	45
7:10	61
14:21	45
27:4	46

Isaiah

5:20	46
6:9–10	79
8:19	42
30:1	46,95
35:8	12
47:13–14	42,46
53:6	31
55:6–7	82
62:5	117

Jeremiah

1:4–5	40
2:13	101
5:3–4	46
13:23	8
16:12	47
17:5	47
17:9	99
23:10	39
31:31–34	25,107

Joel

2:13	25,78

Habakkuk

1:13	21
2:9	47
2:20	73

Malachi

2:16	47
3:8–9	48

Matthew

3:11–12	75,122,126
5:22	48
5:28	48
5:48	13,18,119,127,128
6:1–4,16–18	48,113
6:13	26
7:1–5	49
7:23	74
10:32–33	49
10:38	119
11:30	74
13:41–42	4

APPENDIX B
GLOSSARY OF TERMS INDEX

- I have given simplified definitions here for general understanding of biblical usage or how the terms are used in theological jargon. Page numbers are provided for context in the presentation of this book. Definitions of terms are not always given here but dictionary understanding is assumed.

- I have tried to express this list of sins in terms of nouns; however, the Bible often expresses sin as an adjective. Also, many sins are expressed as opposites of godliness which become sin once a person knows the difference. Sin, like holiness, has no existence outside of relationship with God and man. The page numbers will direct the reader to the scripture which makes the sin known. If nothing else, this listing shows the futility of listing sins to avoid. Obviously ones only way to avoid sin is to be changed by God deep within. It is of great value to see the principle of sin under which all of these fit. Principles we have expressed in Part II are Ignorance, Unbelief (Doubt), Disobedience, Rebellion and Perversion. Redemption and Sanctification not only cover the sin and forgive it, but address the sin principle that causes us to sin in the first place.)

Sin Listing (cont.):

Jesting, coarse -   59

Inventors of evil -   54

Judgment of others -   49

Kidnapping –   40,51

Lawlessness -   66

Lesbianism –   40

Lewdness -   55,57

Love of the world –   66

Lust of the eyes -   48,60

Lust of the flesh – (see Sexual immorality)   55,59

Lying – (see deceit)   39,40,44,45,49,54,64,69

Making children pass through fire – (see Occult)   42

Malice – (Maliciousness)   60,65

Medium, using a – (see Occult)

Misery, causing –   54

Mocking -   68

Money, love of –   62,63

Murder -   39,49,50,60,68,69

Not acting from faith –   55

Not Fearing God –   54

Not giving to the needy -   67

Not keeping the Sabbath -   39

Not loving good –   63

Obscene talk -   60

Occult – witchcraft, soothsayer, omens, sorcery, spells, using a medium, familiar spirits, calling up the dead, astrology -   42

Omens, interpreting – (see Occult)   42

Oppressing the helpless –   44

Orgies –   57,58

Parents, disobedience, dishonoring, striking - 39,43,54,60,63

Sin Listing (cont.):

1. Have other gods before Me
2. Make a carved image and bow down to it
3. Take the Lord's name in vain
4. Ignore the Sabbath

5. Dishonor your father and mother
6. Murder
7. Commit Adultery
8. Steal
9. Bear false witness
10. Covet

Total depravity – There are none who are good   23,79

Unconditional Election – Calvinism's belief that men
    have no say in whether they are elected to be saved   23

ABOUT THE AUTHOR

Paul M. Ethington was born in 1946 in Illinois to a bi-vocational pastor- musician- school teacher, Oakley Ethington. Raised in the Midwest, educated in California and Alaska, in and around the Church of the Nazarene, he developed a deep love for the Scriptures. For the last five decades he has conducted Bible Studies in small groups almost continuously.

Squarely in the middle of orthodox Christianity he may be described as Wesleyan and evangelical. He obtained his B.S. in philosophy and M.S. in music from Cal State Fullerton. Although his vocation has been electrician, he is an avid reader whose hobby is biblical theology and whose passion is teaching. His habit of preparing his own curriculum and materials has led to several books. His penchant for taking complex material and organizing it for ease of understanding makes him very readable. He challenges his students to know Jesus more deeply as they go through life. He is not afraid to ask hard questions and to discuss Bible difficulties. His intention is to be more clear than clever and his style is expositional. He admits that he does not know everything, and that drives him to be an avid student who reads others' work. Yet, he is convinced that the Word of God is accessible to all, and that remains his primary reference and focus; what do the Scriptures say? Mr. Ethington says that experience is instructive though skewed. Tradition is important though selective. Logic and conceptual analysis are helpful though subject to artful manipulation. There is no distinction between science and faith based on evidence. Only the Scriptures by the teaching of the Holy Spirit are completely trustworthy. With thorough exegesis Paul Ethington is determined to communicate this teaching to hungry hearts by the help of the Holy Spirit. He lives in Northern Idaho now with his wife Maria. Having spent most of their lives in SoCal and three years in Alaska, they are enjoying the four seasons. He has two grown children, Marisol and David. Both of them are solid Christians active in their local settings. Still, there is a larger family who Mr. Ethington enjoys wherever he goes who love the Lord and look forward to His coming. His love for music allowed him to lead singing for forty years in the Church of the Nazarene. His love for people causes him to reach outside the walls of the church with frequent visits to missions where he plays the piano, sings and gives his testimony and presents the Word for the encouragement of all who seek Jesus.

www.ingramcontent.com/pod-product-compliance
Lightning Source LLC
Chambersburg PA
CBHW071950150726
47999CB00001B/384